A COMPLETE INTRODUCTION TO
CANARIES

Roller canary pair with just-fledged youngsters.

Young color-fed canaries in the course of molting.

A COMPLETE INTRODUCTION TO

CANARIES

COMPLETELY ILLUSTRATED IN FULL COLOR

Al David

Photographs: . Archiv Klinik für Geflügel TiHo Hannover, 107. L. Arnall, 112, 113, 114, 116. Chelman & Petrulla, 24. Patricia Demko, 18–19, 76, 126–127. Michael Gilroy, 7, 58–59, 66, 67, 69, 71, 73, 74, 78, 91, 95, 96, 98, 101, 102, 103, 118, 122. Michael W. Gos, 25. Ray Hanson, 26. Dr. M. Heidenreich, 120. Dr. I. F. Keymer, 121. Dr. Kummerfeld, Klinik für Geflügel TiHo Hannover, 110, 111. Harry V. Lacey, 2–3, 5, 27, 43, 45, 49, 51, 56, 68, 80, 82, 83, 86–87. Donald Perez, 105. Mervin F. Roberts, 22, 23, 30–31, 35, 44 top, 48, 50, 52, 53, 54–55, 61, 63, 106. W. A. Starika, 64. Louise Van der Meid, 37, 39. Courtesy Vogelpark Walsrode, 57, 65, 85, 92. Wayne Wallace, 33.

Distributed in the UNITED STATES by T.F.H. Publications, Inc., 211 West Sylvania Avenue, Neptune City, NJ 07753; in CANADA to the Pet Trade by H & L Pet Supplies Inc., 27 Kingston Crescent, Kitchener, Ontario N2B 2T6; Rolf C. Hagen Ltd., 3225 Sartelon Street, Montreal 382 Quebec; in CANADA to the Book Trade by Macmillan of Canada (A Division of Canada Publishing Corporation), 164 Commander Boulevard, Agincourt, Ontario M1S 3C7; in ENGLAND by T.F.H. Publications Limited, 4 Kier Park, Ascot, Berkshire SL5 7DS; in AUSTRALIA AND THE SOUTH PACIFIC by T.F.H. (Australia) Pty. Ltd., Box 149, Brookvale 2100 N.S.W., Australia; in NEW ZEALAND by Ross Haines & Son, Ltd., 18 Monmouth Street, Grey Lynn, Auckland 2 New Zealand; in SINGAPORE AND MALAYSIA by MPH Distributors (S) Pte., Ltd., 601 Sims Drive, #03/07/21, Singapore 1438; in the PHILIPPINES by Bio-Research, 5 Lippay Street, San Lorenzo Village, Makati Rizal; in SOUTH AFRICA by Multipet Pty. Ltd., 30 Turners Avenue, Durban 4001. Published by T.F.H. Publications Inc. Manufactured in the United States of America by T.F.H. Publications, Inc.

Contents

Canaries - Their Past And Present

A small finch initially confined to the Azores and Canary Islands was the original ancestor of all the breeds of domestic canary now kept throughout the world. Wild canaries *(Serinus c. canarius)* can still be found on these islands, but bear little resemblance to the birds seen today. They are relatively small, being about 11.5 cm (4½ in) in length and predominantly greenish in color, with darker markings on the upper parts.

Domestication Of The Wild Canary

The Spaniards began the process of domestication during the late fifteenth century, after the Portuguese had first brought these birds to Europe. The canary has been popular since that time by virtue of its song, and German fanciers initially bred birds for this feature. Other European breeders, particularly in Holland and Belgium, concentrated on producing different types of canaries. During subsequent years, British breeds began coming to the fore from the 1850's onward.

Color has always been a feature of canaries, with pure white birds being known as early as 1709. Yellow-colored canaries are another popular mutation, said to have occurred following the wrecking of a ship with a cargo which included wild

Below: *The canary has lent its name to a shade of yellow, and many people think of a canary as a yellow bird.*

canaries. These birds were released, and some reached a nearby island, where they bred with native finches to produce yellow offspring. During this century, in the search

Below: *The coloration of the wild canary is very like that of its close Continental relative, the Common Serin,* Serinus serinus.

for a red canary, Red Factor Canaries have been created by hybridization with a South American finch.

A separate hobby has arisen from canary breeding, and this is the production of mules. These generally result from the pairing of a native cock finch to a hen canary, with Norwich Fancy birds currently being popular for this purpose. Linnet mules for example make good songsters, but Goldfinch mules are often more colorful. It is curious that in the case of the Bullfinch *(Pyrrhula pyrrhula)*, only hens can be used for muling, with cock canaries needed for a successful outcome. All such offspring are unlikely to be fertile, whereas in the case of the Red Factor

A depiction of only some of the canary varieties: (1) Clear Yellow Norwich, (2) Ticked Yellow Border, (3) Green Gloster Corona, (4) Buff Gloster Corona, (5) Green Yorkshire, (6) Yellow Gloster Consort, (7) Scotch Fancy, (8) Dutch Frill, (9) Red-orange Red Factor, (10) Broken-cap Silver Lizard, (11) Clear-cap Gold Lizard, (12) Clear-body Dark Crested.

Canary, the problem of infertility was soon overcome. Having bred now for many generations, they are just as prolific as most breeds, and more so than some.

Pet Canaries

While any cock canary will sing, Rollers are preferred by many people throughout Europe, while the American Singer is a breed gaining popularity as a household bird in the United States. Canaries cannot be taught to talk like budgerigars, but the odd talented mimic is occasionally reported. They may live for over ten years, and are not difficult to maintain in good health.

It is not, however, an easy matter for the inexperienced to identify a cock bird, because there is no obvious difference between the sexes outside the breeding season. At this time, the vent of a cock is slightly enlarged and appears more prominent compared to that of a hen. Blowing the vent feathers aside while the canary is held in the hand is thus the standard way of detecting its sex. When they are not in breeding condition, cocks may still be recognized by their song, although during the molt they will generally stop singing for a period.

Cages And Accessories

Any cage used to house a canary should be

Above: *The trace of yellow in the flights suggests that this Norwich canary is a Dominant White.*

washed well, rinsed thoroughly and dried when it is first obtained, before the bird is placed in it. Wire-type cages are normally used for pet

Below: *Though canaries do remarkably well in quite small cages, it is preferable to house them in cages larger than this.*

canaries, and designs with separate plastic bottoms, available in a range of colors, are preferable, as these are easy to keep clean. This floor unit can be detached, while the removable sand tray is slid into the bottom of the wire top, thus preventing the canary from escaping into the room itself.

A large cage is best, as the canary will benefit from the extra space available. It is unwise to let these birds fly free into a room because they do not return to their cages as readily as do budgerigars, and may well prove difficult to recapture. Many breeders use a well-padded net to catch their stock when required. The cage should be positioned on a firm stand away from direct sunlight or drafts.

Most cages have perches included with them, but these may need to be altered to offer some variety in diameter. A square perch or a suitable branch are possible alternatives. These should be positioned in the cage so that the canary's tail does not rub against the bars. A bird-bath which fits on the cage door will also be of benefit in keeping the plumage in good condition.

Covered feeders are not immediately accepted by all birds, and at first a little seed should be sprinkled on the floor in front of the main supply, as with grit. Water is most conveniently provided by means of a plastic drinker which clips on to the cage bars. Other foods can be given in separate containers hooked on the sides of the cage or placed on the floor. Seed wastage can be a problem with some canaries, and apart from offering every type of seed separately, the only alternative is to put clean seed from the floor back into the feeding dish. There are special machines known as winnowers used by breeders for separating good seed from chaff, but these are not likely to be economical for pet owners.

Aviaries

Canaries make attractive aviary birds, either on their own or living alongside small foreign finches such as Waxbills *(Estrilda spp.)*. They can also be kept with Cockatiels *(Nymphicus hollandicus),* and sometimes safely with Grass Parakeets *(Neophema spp.)* without being bullied; however breeding

Above: *If a cage is to be situated on a windowsill, take care that the canary can avoid the direct sunlight if it wishes to.*

results are more successful when they are housed on their own, or bred in cages. Canaries should not be kept with other parrot-

Below: *Outside the breeding season, canaries housed in a flight profit from the opportunity for exercise.*

like birds, such as budgerigars, as they are likely to be attacked, and will not be able to defend themselves.

An aviary for canaries need not be an expensive structure. They are hardy birds, and as a rule do not require artificial heating or lighting during the winter months in temperate climates. The aviary should, however, be located in a sheltered position, but not overhung by trees, which will reduce the available light on a winter's day, with the possibility of leaves and branches falling on the structure itself.

Obtaining Stock

The source of stock will vary according to the requirements of the purchaser. For those who are interested in the exhibition side of the hobby, it is essential to make contact with experienced, reputable sellers. Apart from supplying canaries, such people are often ready to assist the newcomer, discussing the various points and faults in a bird, for example. It is also important to join the relevant specialist society, which exists for all the various breeds. The current address of the appropriate secretary can be

Below: *Border canary varieties: Dilute Blue above and Dilute Fawn below.*

obtained through the various bird-keeping journals, as well as much useful advice and advertisements of stock. There are also many local clubs throughout the country, so it is relatively easy to meet other breeders in the neighborhood.

Showing

Most clubs have their own annual shows for members only, whereas anyone can enter birds at an Open show. Every canary must be benched in the appropriate show cage for that particular breed. Such cages differ in dimensions and design, and strict rules are enforced to ensure there is no variation in this respect. Exhibitors start as novices and, by virtue of their wins, progress to champion status. Once this has been achieved, it is not permissible to revert to novice status even if showing another breed.

The initial step is to obtain the show schedule and entry form from the show secretary. The schedule lists all the classes and

Above: *Type-canary champions at the 1981 National Institute of Red Orange Canaries (NIROC) show held in Illinois, where a Yorkshire canary received the top award.*

should be read carefully before the entry form is completed. Any incorrect entries will result in subsequent disqualification at the show.

Cage labels will be sent out prior to the show, after the entries have been received. The birds themselves should be benched as early as possible, so they can settle down after their journey. Water is given after judging at local shows, so the container must not be filled beforehand. There is a risk that the canary may get its plumage wet and thus spoil its chances at this late stage. After the awards have been made, it is advantageous to study the other birds in the classes, noting their strengths and weaknesses. Most judges are happy to discuss an exhibitor's entries and offer advice when approached.

Aviaries And Birdrooms

There is a variety of possible options for keeping canaries outdoors. A simple aviary with dry and draft-free roosting quarters is all that is required in the first instance. It may even be possible to build a small flight on to an existing wall close to the house, where the birds' song and color can be fully appreciated. However, it is best to consult with the local government to learn what, if any, building restrictions exist in your area.

Aviaries

Suitable aviaries for canaries can be obtained from firms advertising in the bird-keeping magazines. Alternatively, it is possible to purchase individual panels and thus design an aviary to meet one's personal requirements. Further development will then

Below: *In the typical aviary an enclosure of wire known as a "flight" communicates with a solidly enclosed room, the "shelter."*

simply entail the addition of extra panels to the existing structure.

Serious breeders will aim for a combined aviary and birdroom, which affords space for suitable cages, seed storage and perhaps even an inside flight.

Building An Aviary Flight

A framework of 3.75 cm (1½ in) square timber forms a suitable basis for an aviary flight. A convenient size is 2.7 metres in length, 0.9 metres wide and 1.8 metres high (9 x 3 x 6 ft.). For an outside

Working on these principles, in areas where space or climate does not permit an outside aviary, breeders often convert a spare room for their birds. Successful results can be obtained under such conditions, although this is perhaps not an ideal set-up.

Above: *Here outdoor flights have been built onto a house. The windows permit birds housed no doubt in an indoor flight to be let outdoors as the weather allows.*

location, this should be painted with a wood preservative. It is best to apply the preservative to the lengths of wood before they are actually assembled to form a frame, but after jointing, so that all exposed cuts are treated with

Above: *This small flight allows the birds relief from the temperatures likely to occur in an upper story on a summer's day.*

preservative. Jointing the frames will give the finished structure increased stability. After being left to dry thoroughly for three weeks, the frames can be made up, as the wood will then be safe for the canaries.

Aviary Netting Wire netting 90 cm (3 ft) in width is most convenient, as this fits the dimensions of the flight outlined earlier, with no wastage. Three lengths of just over 180 cm (6 ft) will be required for each side unit, with the supporting bars being at intervals of 90 cm (3 ft) apart, as in the case of the roof section. The wire can be of 19 gauge, with mesh dimensions of preferably 1.25 by 1.25 cm (1/2 x 1/2 in), to keep out even the smallest mice. Failing this, mesh of 1.25 x 2.5 cm (1/2 x 1 in) can be used.

Netting of this size and gauge will also suffice for any small finches and even cockatiels living with the canaries. If only small seed-eaters are to be

their companions, green plastic coated wire mesh can be used to cover the frames. This looks quite attractive and often has a longer lifespan than standard galvanized wire.

Below: *Custom-sized cages and flights may be constructed of wire mesh. The pieces are fastened together with sheet-metal "clips" installed by means of specially designed pliers.*

Discount suppliers of aviary netting advertise regularly, and slightly damaged rolls are often available at even larger reductions. Chicken wire of a suitable mesh diameter is also quite suitable for use on canary aviaries, but being virtually circular rather than square or rectangular, it is difficult to cut in a straight line leaving no loose ends.

easiest to start at one pair of corners before fixing the opposite pair, as this should ensure that the netting remains taut on the frame and does not sag. A slight overlap top and bottom enables the cut ends to be bent over and attached to the adjoining face, where they will be out of reach once the frames are assembled.

For wiring purposes, the frames should be laid on a flat, horizontal surface. U-shaped netting staples applied at regular intervals around the frame are most suitable for attaching the wire. It is

Above: *The service corridor between two rows of flights permits access to each for feeding and cleaning. Note that in this facility the corridor is also roofed with wire mesh.*

The Shelter

A similar basic framework, but sloping from front to back, can be constructed for the shelter. The outer surface needs to be clad in tongued-and-grooved wood, treated with a preservative, or marine plywood. The interior sides of the shelter frames can be wired over, with loose ends protected by thin battening, or covered by oil-tempered hardboard. This material, painted with a light emulsion can be wiped over as necessary, and dirt cannot accumulate behind the lining as with wire netting. It also affords some insulation, but mice can establish themselves behind this lining, if they gain access to the aviary.

Above: *The rear of this outdoor flight is roofed solid and paneled on the sides. Only in a warm climate would this degree of shelter be suitable for canaries.*

Entrances A door with a window should be located in the back of the shelter. The glass must, however, be wired over to deter any birds from attempting to fly through it. The light thus made available will encourage the canaries to enter the shelter, and also serves to make inspection easier. Another door leading from the shelter into the flight will also be necessary.

A connecting hole with a platform, giving the canaries adequate access to and from the shelter, should be

25

Above: *A flight designed for a colder climate: the wired areas can be fitted with panes during the winter.*

located high up adjoining this second door. By means of a sliding runner, in which sits a suitable piece of plywood attached to thick wire passing out through the aviary mesh, it is possible to close the entrance from outside the aviary. The shelter can then be entered safely if all the canaries are shut out in the flight. Some may be reluctant to leave however, particularly at feeding time and so a safety porch is often included in the design of many canary aviaries.

The porch itself is located either at the back of the shelter or more commonly around an entrance at the end of the flight. In the latter instance, the rear shelter door is therefore not essential, unlike the window, which then has to be built into the structure itself and should again be removable, for ventilation purposes. Construction of the safety porch is on the same lines as for the flight. The outer door is closed before the aviary

Above: *Controlled canary breeding requires a battery of cages in which hens and cocks may be paired specifically. In this bird room, removable partitions allow the spaces to be allocated as needed: the small enclosures of the breeding season become flights for the rest of the year.*

itself is entered, so that no canary can fly straight out and be lost as a result.

Foundations For The Aviary

The whole structure should be mounted on a solid brick foundation, extending 15 cm (6 in) above ground level, and at least 30 cm (1 ft) beneath the surface. This will serve to keep rats out, which otherwise may kill or

maim the canaries and also prevents the aviary woodwork from rotting.

The bolts which will attach the frames to the base should be set firmly in mortar between the bricks and corresponding holes drilled in the frames. It is useful to apply washers before the nuts, because then, with regular oiling, the sections can be easily taken down and moved or altered as required.

Protection From The Elements The flight itself should be covered on the roof and sides with translucent plastic sheeting for a distance

Above: Permanance in bird buildings can best be achieved by masonry construction, partricularly for the foundations that support the framing over which the wire mesh is spread.

of about 90 cm (3 ft), which can then be attached to the first set of supporting bars. This will give the canaries protection during bad weather.

In order to ensure that the shelter remains dry, the roof can be tarred, and any small gaps should be filled out of reach of the canaries with a suitable preparation. Heavy duty roofing felt should then be fixed on top, preferably as a double layer. Guttering running along the back edge will channel off rainwater, which can be usefully passed to a garden water-butt.

Floor Coverings The canaries will spend some time picking around the aviary floor, looking for spilled seeds and even suitable nesting material. A solid base for both the flight and shelter is therefore preferable, as it can be cleaned thoroughly and even washed off as required. Concrete is most suitable, but should be laid to a depth of at least 10 cm (4 in), sloping in the flight towards the front, where a small hole is located for drainage purposes. Setting wire netting into this floor covering will act as a further deterrent to rats and

Above: *A double-breeder cage with a wire partition. The nest pans (only one is needed), also made of wire, can easily be cleaned thoroughly.*

other burrowing vermin.

A grass floor in the flight may appear attractive initially, but soon becomes unsightly, especially if the shelter has to be entered daily via the flight. Waterlogging often occurs during periods of wet weather, and moss will then predominate in place of grass.

Coarse gravel can be raked over at intervals but, as with a grass floor, is extremely difficult to keep clean. Paving slabs infilled with mortar are, however, useful as a more temporary measure than concrete, but have the same advantages.

Perches The perches should be of a variable diameter, taken from woods which are not likely to be poisonous, such as sycamore, elderberry and apple. They must be washed off before being used, and should never be cut from trees which have recently been sprayed. Perches of yew, lilac and laburnum are best avoided as they may prove toxic.

Dowelling perches, preferably planed to a more oval or square shape rather than the normal round conformation should be confined to the shelter, as the canaries need to exercise their feet on

wood of different thicknesses. These can be fixed in place with brackets, while those in the outside flight can be attached to the framework by loops of wire. All perches should be placed across the aviary, rather than running lengthwise, and must not overhang each other, as the lower branches will soon be soiled with bird droppings.

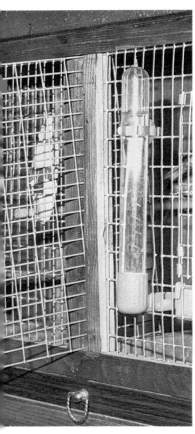

Above: *A heavier gauge wire mesh is stiff enough that a piece to serve as a partition need only be cut to size.*

Breeding Cages

Suitable cages can be purchased ready for use, but may need painting with an emulsion paint. Lead-based paints should be avoided as these are potentially poisonous. It is also possible to build breeding cages using thin plywood, or hardboard. A basic rectangular design will be adequate, and cage fronts are available in a variety of sizes.

A double breeding cage with a removable center partition is most useful. Each unit should be about 45 cm (18 in) long, and 30 cm in height and depth (1 ft), working in conjunction with the size of the cage front. A sliding tray must be incorporated below this for cleaning purposes. The floor itself can be lined with old newspaper, while sawdust is popular with some fanciers because of its absorbent qualities. Two perches running across each cage from back to front will be required and these should be of different shapes, so the canaries have to exercise their feet as a result. Having decided on the dimensions for a cage, it will be much easier if these are maintained for all subsequent cages.

Feeding

Seed forms the major part of a canary's diet, but it is deficient in some respects. For this reason, egg food, greenfood and even grit are all of benefit to the birds. The essential components of various foods offered to canaries, excluding vitamin and mineral levels, are shown in the table.

Seed Types

The seeds in this table fall into two main categories. Millet and canary seed (Phalaris canariensis) are cereals obtained from various grasses. They contain relatively high proportions of carbohydrate, which is used by the body primarily to meet its energy requirements. Millet is rarely fed to canaries nowadays but will be eaten in a communal aviary, as it is often the main constituent of finch seed mixtures. Canary seed however, forms the basis of most mixtures for these birds. There are various strains available, of which Mazagan grown in Morocco is popularly regarded as the best. Canadian and Australian crops are also sold on the world market, and some British canary seed is offered each year, although in smaller

Relative Nutritional Values of Selected Seeds

Food	Fat	Carbohydrate	Protein	Water
Rape Seed	40.0	20.0	22.0	7.0
Hemp	30.0	25.0	16.0	11.0
Maw Seed	45.0	18.0	19.0	9.0
Niger	40.0	22.0	21.0	12.0
Linseed	34.0	23.0	23.0	9.0
Millet	5.0	56.0	14.0	15.0
Canary Seed	4.0	55.0	17.0	14.0
Dandelion	1.0	10.6	2.4	84.0
Carrot	0.1	9.6	1.2	87.0
Lettuce	0.2	2.0	1.0	95.0
Apple	–	15.0	0.5	83.0
Egg white	0.25	–	10.0	87.0
Egg yolk	33.0	–	15.0	47.0

quantities.

The other seeds in this list are classed as oil seeds because of their high fat levels. Fat is a concentrated source of energy, apart from having more specific functions such as forming an integral part of all cell membranes in the body. Rape seed (*Brassica rapa*) is available in several forms, notably black, red and German Rubsen. The latter variety in particular is often fed to Rollers, as it is thought to encourage them to sing better. Red rape forms the basis of most seed mixtures however, while the black type is often soaked before feeding.

Hemp *(Cannabis sativa)* is the relatively large brownish seed in a good quality mixture. It is a source of the stimulant drug cannabis,

Right: *Pet shops make seeds available separately and in mixes. The open wicker nests (pans) are for canaries, the closed ones for finches.*

and early breeders fed a relatively high proportion of this seed to keep their birds singing well. Hemp is generally the most popular seed with canaries, but now offered only in restricted amounts during the year, apart from the breeding season, when it is often crushed or soaked before feeding.

Niger *(Guizotia abyssinica)* is a thin blackish seed derived from an annual plant which resembles a daisy. It can be grown in temperate countries, obtaining a maximum height of 180 cm (6 ft) but is easily killed by frost. Prices have risen steeply in recent years, largely because of crop failures in growing areas such as North India. Niger is often fed prior to the breeding season, as it is felt to decrease the occurrence of egg-binding.

Maw seed derived from poppies *(Papaver somniferum)* occurs in blue and white varieties. The former is especially popular, marketed as Dutch Blue Maw Seed. It is the sap present in the developing seed-head and not the seed itself which is used to produce opium and its derivatives. The seeds are dispersed through the top of the pod, which lifts off when they are ripe. A popular tonic seed, of particular value for convalescing and molting canaries, maw is often sprinkled on top of soft food or bread and milk.

Linseed *(Linum usitattisimum)* is also valuable during the molting period and helps

Above: *Spray millet provides occupation as well as food value for a canary, but usually none of the millets are staples of a canary diet.*

Above: *For small enclosures, the tubular water font is favored by many canary owners and breeders. It can be installed so that servicing can be accomplished from outside the cage.*

to ensure that the new plumage has a good bloom. This flat, brown seed is not generally a favorite with most canaries however, and may be ignored in a mixture. Gold of pleasure *(Camelina sativa)* is another tonic seed used by some breeders.

A seed which has become very popular as a rearing food in recent years is Teazle *(Dipsacus sylvestris),* although it is very expensive. The plant grows wild in certain parts of the country however, and can be cultivated without difficulty in a garden. Its main drawback is that it reaches a size of several feet, both in width and height.

A variety of other wild seeds can be gathered and fed to canaries, either fresh or dried.

Plantain *(Plantago major)* also known as Rat's Tail, is readily taken by most birds, although not available commercially. It helps to ensure a good molt when offered as the seeds are ripening, turning from green to brown. As with all wild plants fed to livestock though, plantain must not be gathered from roadside shoulders or other areas where weedkillers or insecticides may have contaminated the herbage. It can be stored for winter use by drying the seed heads upside down in a damp-free location, ensuring that they show no trace of mold.

Greenfood

Seeding grasses of various types, such as Meadow Grass *(Poa annua)* are greedily taken by most birds. Chickweed *(Stellaria media)* is also used by many breeders, who offer it on a regular basis, but particularly when chicks are being reared. Dandelion *(Taraxacum officinale)*

Above: *The seeds ordinarily fed dry may also be planted in saucers. When they have grown sufficiently, the saucers may be placed in the flight, where they will provide the inhabitants with greenfood.*

leaves or roots are also of great value, containing a relatively high proportion of minerals. The roots can be washed off thoroughly and cut into pieces or crushed and their juice mixed with the drinking water, given

may be fed, providing they are unaffected by frost. Greenfood should be washed thoroughly and shaken dry to remove excessive moisture before being given to the birds. Some canaries, especially those living indoors, will roll about on damp greenfood to wet their feathers.

Sweet apple and carrot are other possible additions to a canary's diet, but care should be taken when feeding carrots because their juice contains a natural coloring agent which can alter the subsequent appearance of a molting canary.

weekly as a tonic. The water must as always be changed every day however, and the container washed out afterwards.

Cultivated crops such as fresh lettuce with its seed-heads and spinach beet can also be offered when wild foods are in short supply. The latter plant will provide greenfood throughout the year, while in the winter particularly, various forms of cabbage, such as Brussels sprouts,

Vitamins And Minerals

Greenfood and carrots will help to correct any deficiency of Vitamin A in the stock, which is likely to arise if the canaries are fed a diet of seed alone. The Vitamin A content falls rapidly after harvesting, but it has an important role in protecting the body against infections.

Vitamin D_3 is another vitamin of considerable importance, particularly in growing and breeding canaries since it controls the calcium levels of the body. It is formed by the ultra-violet component of sunlight falling on the correct vitamin and mineral deficiencies, but these must be used in accordance with the given instructions, as an excess may be equally harmful. The most

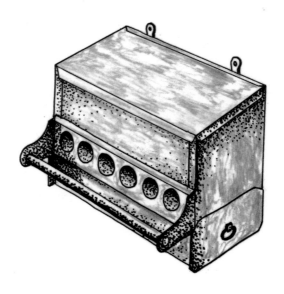

Above: *A seed hopper made of sheet metal. The feeding holes are designed to prevent the birds from scattering seeds as they search for their favorite kinds.*

feathers, and so canaries kept inside are likely to be deficient in this respect.

There are various tonics available to comprehensive preparations also contain essential amino acids such as lysine. Powder may be sprinkled on seed but is more likely to be consumed if mixed with soft food or greenfood, while some brands are available in liquid form and dispensed via the birds' drinking water.

Grit And Cuttlefish Bone

These are both important sources of minerals, while grit is also vital for the digestive system. Seed passes from the crop, where it is stored, into the gizzard, and here the muscular walls of this organ combine with the rough edges of mineralized grit to break down the food into smaller particles. In comparison oystershell grit is quite soluble and will dissolve in the acid medium of the gizzard, liberating minerals which are then absorbed. Sea sand should be mixed with oystershell, which together will help to ensure supplies of vital minerals like iodine.

Cuttlefish bone is also obtained indirectly from the sea. It comes from a marine mollusc, and these white bones can occasionally be found washed up on beaches, usually after storms. Although they may be over 30 cm (1 ft) long,

Below: Cuttlefish bones and mineral blocks provide the minerals caged canaries need.

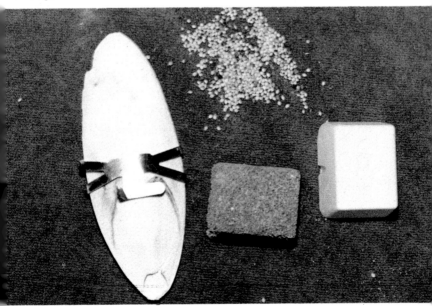

Border canaries. The recessive white mutation produces the greatest absence of pigment. In the Blue, the melanin markings are still present on the white ground color.

Above: *Outside baths are designed to hang on the wire over the open door.*

size is unimportant, while in fact broken bones are generally cheaper and can be purchased from seed merchants. Those collected on the beach should be cleaned off as necessary and then washed thoroughly at home before being left to dry. Any which are polluted with tar must never be offered to the birds.

Canaries may have difficulty in nibbling at a whole bone, so for this reason cutting off smaller pieces from the soft side is recommended.

Cuttlefish must always be available to them, like grit, throughout the year, although more will be consumed during the breeding season. The calcium present in these bones will be required for the eggshells and subsequent bone development of the chicks.

Soft Foods
There is a variety of commercially prepared soft foods now available in packaged form, but some fanciers prefer to use their own recipes. The major ingredient added to some soft foods is egg, fed for its protein content. Egg biscuit mixtures are, however, more

economical and simpler to use than feeding hard-boiled eggs chopped up into small pieces and mixed with breadcrumbs, moistened with equal volumes of water and milk.

Each protein is comprised of a series of amino acid residues, certain of which are essential and cannot be synthesized in the body. Seeds and other forms of vegetable protein are relatively deficient in these essential amino acids, such as lysine, and so supplementation with animal protein is required to prevent a deficiency. The body's demands for such protein are increased during growth and molting phases, as well as in the breeding season.

Color Food

The origins of color feeding can be traced back to the 1870's, when a fancier fed some cayenne pepper to one of his Norwich Fancy bird which was poorly during the molt. The canary's plumage became deep orange and subsequently in the next year, following similar treatment, he was able to bench birds with the same depth of color. In spite of objections, analysis could not detect the means of coloration, but it became known in 1873. The varieties now color-fed for exhibition purposes, apart from the Norwich, are the Lizard, Yorkshire, and Red Factor Canaries.

Above: *Many cage cups are designed to attach to the cage wire, which permits servicing from outside the cage.*

Red Factor canaries are able to metabolize foodstuffs into red pigments. However, with some color foods the resulting color is by many fanciers castigated as excessive and unnatural looking.

Above: *As seed eaters, canaries are naturally inclined to feed from the floor; however, this arrangement may not be sufficiently hygienic.*

Below: *Foods that are fed in small amounts may be offered in special utensils known as "treat cups."*

The coloring agent can be obtained ready-mixed, in the form of a color food, or as a liquid to add to the drinking water. This concentrated coloring agent needs to be mixed with care however, as an excess will result in poor, unnatural coloration and red droppings. For this reason, the use of a prepared color food may be more satisfactory for the novice canary owner. Red Factor Canaries can be given their special blend or even 'Carophyll Red' directly in the water as they need to be a deeper color than the other varieties.

Feeding During The Molt

In the northern hemisphere, canaries normally begin molting towards the end of July, through to September. The developing feathers initially have a blood supply, and by this route the coloring agent reaches the plumage. It is usually fed just before molting starts, up until several weeks after no new feathers are apparent, and even longer in some cases. A fixed quantity should be offered regularly on a daily basis throughout this period to ensure that a good even color is produced.

Once the blood supply ceases, it is impossible to improve the bird's color artificially. Continuing with color feeding once a week after the molt however, should ensure that any odd replacement feathers will be of matching color. With molting stock, it is useful to offer as wide a range of food as possible at this time, especially valuable sources of protein such as hard-boiled egg or milk diluted 50:50 with water. A general tonic is also

Above: *This Buff Norwich cock shows the effects of color feeding, which is sometimes practiced in the Norwich fancy.*

beneficial and should help to get the birds through the molt as quickly as possible.

45

General Feeding Principles

Every fancier has his/her own method of feeding their canaries. A standard seed mixture comprised of three parts canary seed and one part rape with small amounts of the other seeds added forms a good basis. The birds must never be deprived of seed or water: the amount consumed by each individual is obviously variable, depending on factors

Above: *A matchstick or the like is a quite suitable tool for hand-rearing a canary—in this instance, a Lizard youngster.*

such as the external temperature, but a daily intake of about 5g of seed and 1g of soft food for each bird could be considered average.

All foodstuffs used must be free from mold, and seed should never be damp or musty. Any seed contaminated with rodents' droppings must be avoided at all costs, as this represents a considerable disease hazard. Most fanciers store their seed in metal tins or bins so that it cannot be fouled by rats or mice in the vicinity. Special safe traps are now available to eliminate such pests if they gain access to the canaries' surroundings.

Variety is perhaps the key to success in keeping canaries fit and healthy. A range of greenfood can be offered throughout the year, as well as soft food, from which the birds will benefit. Feeding during the breeding season is considered in the next chapter, being an integral part of management at this time.

Breeding

Canaries will usually start breeding at the beginning of April in northern climates or slightly earlier if the weather has been mild. Their breeding cycle is also influenced by day length, with an increase setting off a complex series of events culminating in reproductive behavior. For this reason, prolonged use of artificial light in a birdroom is not recommended, as it can interfere with the natural chain of events.

The canaries themselves must also be in good condition to breed successfully, and feeding plays a very important part. Some breeders do not offer soft foods until after the chicks have hatched, but the use of this and condition seed mixtures containing niger as well as greenfood can be of benefit beforehand. Indeed, the developing chicks themselves are dependent on the nutrients contained in their eggs, which depends in turn on the hen's diet prior to laying. Any deficiencies at this time, of minerals for example, are likely to lead to poor hatchability.

Preparing For The Breeding Season

In early March, breeding stock should be assessed, and any birds which have overgrown

Above: *A canary hen in a ceramic nest pan, about to settle down to incubate her clutch of eggs.*

Facing page: *Canary eggs, slightly bluish with dark speckling, can vary considerably in size.*

nails will require attention to prevent punctured eggs and even chicks being pulled out accidentally from the nest once breeding gets underway in earnest. A course of treatment for mites is also advisable to reduce the risk of these parasites becoming established. Some breeders also carefully trim any thick feathering extending over the vent, in case this interferes with successful mating.

Cage Breeding

The cages themselves, having been thoroughly cleaned and repainted after the previous season, should be checked over and any needed repairs carried out. It is important that the perches fit firmly for mating to be successful, while the nest pan must also be fixed securely in

Above: *Most nest pans are designed so that they may be installed on the wire or the walls of the cage, off the floor.*

place, using a screw. The pan is generally positioned at the back of the cage, slightly higher than the two perches. Once the cage has been thoroughly dusted with a safe powder to kill mites and the floor lined, preferably with newspaper, the hens can be caught up and placed therein, with one to a cage.

Breeding Accessories

Nest pans today are generally made of plastic, but earthenware and metal receptacles are still in use. The pan forms a suitable hollow in which the hen will build her nest and should be lined with a special felt or a piece of clean sacking or blanket and dusted on both surfaces with a preparation to kill mites.

Nesting material is also required and can be obtained from a pet shop. Dried moss is a popular alternative available from many florists, but is perhaps not as hygienic. The material should be teased out and fixed through the cage bars,

Above: *A canary nest containing four eggs. The nest pan has been fitted with dark felt to form a substrate which the bird lines with fibers, string, and such.*

where the hen will help herself. Alternatively, special racks are available, but in many cases the material ends up on the cage floor.

Dummy eggs of pottery or

plastic will need to be substituted for the hen's eggs as they are laid. When she has finished her clutch, normally on the fourth day after starting to lay, the dummy eggs are removed and her own replaced, thus ensuring that the chicks should hatch together, rather than at intervals of a day, when the youngest are unlikely to survive.

An egg box will be required for storing the eggs until they can be put back into the nest. A suitable storage box may be made with individual compartments or even matchboxes lined with paper tissues or cotton wool on which the eggs will rest are adequate. It is however important, especially with a number of eggs, to replace the correct clutch under the appropriate hen, and some form of numbering, correlating with the pair number for example, is recommended.

Various feeding accessories, apart from the normal containers used for seed and water, are especially valuable during the breeding season. Egg-food drawers and feeding trays to accommodate them are popular and make the task of dispensing rearing foods much

Below: *Dummy eggs, nowadays mostly made of plastic, are substituted for the hen's real eggs.*

Above: *Canary hatchling amid the tow and yarn offered for nesting material.*

easier. A quantity can be mixed and dispensed to individual birds without undue disturbance. With two sets, when fresh food is given in a clean drawer the other can be removed simultaneously for washing later using a mild detergent, followed by a thorough rinse. Scrupulous hygiene with all perishable foods is very important, particularly when there are chicks in the nest.

Mating

There are several ways of introducing the cock to his intended mate. It is however, vital that both birds are ready to breed, because otherwise infertile or 'clear' eggs are likely to result. Pairs should ideally be kept separate therefore, but in close proximity, until they are showing signs of wanting to mate. This can be achieved by housing them in a double breeding cage with the partition drawn slightly back so the birds can see each other, or by housing the cock in a wire cage alongside the hen. Once he starts singing constantly and dancing along the perch, while the hen carries nesting material and solicits feeding with wings outstretched, chirping loudly, the birds can be placed together. After several days the cock should be removed, before his mate has laid. It is possible to run one cock with two or more hens in the course of a season.

Laying

Having built her nest, the hen normally lays about a week to two weeks following the cock's introduction. The greenish-blue eggs are speckled reddish-brown, although these markings are very variable. Most eggs are laid in the morning and should be removed as suggested previously. They must be handled as little as possible, ideally only with clean, washed hands as bacteria on the skin can be transferred and pass through the shell to the developing embryo. Any small cracks visible in the shell can be dabbed over with nail varnish, which should help to ensure they have a better chance of hatching.

Hatching And Rearing

The incubation period is

normally about thirteen days commencing from the day when the eggs were returned to the hen. This is slightly variable however, and may be extended for a further day or so in

Just prior to hatching, the hens should be given a supply of a suitable rearing food with a high egg content. Increasing amounts should then be offered three times daily if possible throughout the rearing period, along with other foods such as soaked seed and greenfood, given on a regular basis. The blend of soft food should not be changed during this time, if at all possible.

Special seed mixtures for soaking are available, while individual seeds such as teazle are also of benefit. A small quantity, sufficient for one feed only, should be covered with hot water, and left standing for twenty-four hours. This treatment stimulates the germination process, making the seed itself more digestible, particularly for young stock. It must be washed off very thoroughly in a sieve before being fed to the canaries.

Hens should never be turned off their nests, but will often come

Above: *A bank of canary breeding cages. Misting with water improves hatching when conditions are insufficiently humid.*

some cases, particularly during cold weather.

down to feed when offered such foods. The nest can be quietly inspected to check and

Below: *A pair of variegated Border canaries at their nest.*

count the number of chicks present. As they grow older, the youngsters sit up to be fed by the hen, from about the tenth day onwards. Once they are about eighteen days old, the cock can be reunited with his mate, to fertilize the second clutch of eggs. It is advisable to provide a clean nest pan, located perhaps at one of the ends of the cage, along with more nesting material for this round. The early chicks should be weaned at the age of three weeks, and the original nest pan can then be removed and cleaned.

Weaning

The young canaries should be removed ideally in the morning, so they have the rest of the day to settle down together in their new surroundings. A feeding tray is particularly valuable at this stage, and the routine also should not be altered.

The normal rearing foods and brown bread and milk sprinkled with maw, as well as soaked seed, must be available. The youngsters may not take the seed at once, but most will start pecking around without difficulty, starting to feed themselves. The cage should be cleaned twice a day so that no stale food can accumulate, and lead to digestive problems. Any birds which appear obviously distressed and fluffed up by the evening will need to be returned to one of the parents, who should feed the young canary, and then the process must be repeated the following day, hopefully with better results. Such movement is not to be recommended however, and may interfere with the hen's second round.

It is usual to introduce hard seed to the canaries when they are about seven weeks old. At their first molt, the body feathers will be

Below: *Canary nestlings beg for food by extending their necks straight up and gaping.*

lost, but not those of the wings and tail. Color feeding should begin in relevant cases, as indicated earlier, just prior to the molt. These young birds are known as unflighted or non-flighted, retaining these paler nest feathers, which will not be molted until the following year.

Upper: *Canary hen incubating: she has settled down on the eggs, adjusting her breast feathers so that the eggs contact her skin directly.*

Lower: *Hatchling canaries are sparsely covered with down and their eyes are still closed.*

Upper: *The speckles and lines marking the eggs are completely variable, the only regularity being that they are concentrated at the blunt end, a conseqence of the mechanics of shell deposition.*

Lower: *As the nestlings grow, the down covering increases.*

For exhibition purposes, they are thus entered in unflighted classes.

Banding

There are two types of ring in current use, available with details such as the breeder's initials, a number to identify the bird concerned and the year.

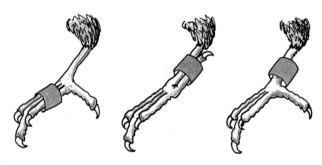

Closed rings are continuous circular bands and have to be applied when the chicks are about six days old, before the foot is too big for the ring to be passed over the individual toes. Instructions on applying these rings are normally sent with the order. Split rings can be put on at any age, being slipped directly over the leg itself, and are a useful means of identifying individuals.

Above: *When the chick is at the right age, the closed ring, or band, will just slip over the foot when the three forward-pointing toes are held together. The rear toe keeps the ring from ever falling off.*

Aviary Breeding

Canaries will generally breed quite well in an aviary, but some bickering is likely, particularly over nesting sites. Twice as many nest pans as hens will therefore be required to reduce the risk of squabbling, and these should all be positioned at the same height under cover. Cocks also can get aggressive during the breeding season and a watch should be kept for any individual which is being persecuted. It is probably advisable to remove young birds for weaning at three weeks and keep them separate, as for stock reared in cages.

Breeding Problems: Desertion

Problems can arise at all stages of the breeding cycle, and disappointment at times is inevitable. Desertion

Canary chicks, like these Border youngsters, often leave the nest before they are fully feathered. As the down feathers continue to grow, they turn into sheathed pennaceous feathers.

is not very common, but when it does occur, the effects can be catastrophic. A disturbance of some kind, especially at night, is likely to cause hens to leave their nests. Flashing lights or mice in close proximity to the birds are just two possible causes. Removing the cock after the hen is sitting may also upset her sufficiently to abandon her eggs.

Failure To Hatch Eggs which fail to hatch may not have been fertilized, and thus can be seen through when viewed in a clear light. The cock may not have been in top condition, so mating was unsuccessful, or he might have been taken away too soon. Dead embryos, which developed but did not

Below: *Three Gloster chicks at fledging age, still a bit too young to feed themselves.*

hatch, can result from chilling of the eggs, genetic factors or a low humidity prior to hatching. Dietary deficiencies can also be responsible. Such losses are referred to as 'death-in-the-shell'. On very rare occasions though, double-yolked eggs have been laid and hatched successfully to yield chicks.

Death In The Nest

Chicks dying in the nest are a sad occurrence. It may be that they were not receiving sufficient food, in which case the youngest are often the first to suffer. Other potential problems, such as nestling diarrhea or 'sweating' are discussed later (along with slipped claw) in the chapter on health problems. If a hen is known to be a poor parent or dies, it is sensible to foster out the eggs to another pair. Chicks can also be switched, but in either case, they should be transferred to a hen at a similar stage in the breeding cycle. This is a major advantage of pairing up all birds at the same time.

Young canaries, generally less than five days old, are sometimes found on the cage floor, having been pulled out of the nest by the hen. They can be revived on occasion, even if they appear dead, by gentle warming in cupped hands for several minutes. Then, after being replaced alongside its nestmates, the youngster should be fed by the hen, whereas if it is left on the floor, the chick will be ignored. Once the young

Above: *Once mostly feathered and therefore no longer in need of brooding, nestlings spend most of their time huddled together.*

canaries are partially feathered, some will leave the nest pan early. They can be replaced, but often hop out again, or overbalance when begging for food.

Feather-plucking Hens will sometimes pluck their chicks just prior to fledging. The cause is often that she is keen to nest again, and if possible they should be transferred to the cock, who will take over the task of rearing the youngsters. Unfortunately, some may then persist with the vice and need to be separated from their nestmates later.

Colors, Markings And Genetics

A canary's color results primarily from the pigments present in its feathers, and modification to the normal pattern of distribution seen in the Wild Canary has given rise to the mutation colors seen today.

Color Pigments

The melanin group of pigments are synthesized by the canary from amino acid residues obtained from the breakdown of protein. There are different pigments involved, being responsible for brown and black coloration.

Below: *A cock Red Siskin, source of the gene that produces red coloration in canaries.*

Melanin itself gives rise to black in the plumage, and the granules are located especially around the feather vanes, as well as in the under feathers. Another pigment, eumelanin brown is associated with melanin here. By way of contrast, a second brown pigment, phaemelanin brown, is found at the edges of the feathers. The absence of all this group of pigments will then result in a pure yellow canary.

The fourth pigment in a canary's plumage is a member of the carotenoid group, called lipochrome, which is fat-soluble and responsible for yellow coloration. Carotenoids occur naturally in plants, and carrot is a rich source of the form known as carotene. This lighter color is normally masked by the melanin pigments, and so may be referred to as the ground color. When lipochrome as well as the melanins are absent from the feathers, then a white form of the canary is produced. There are two forms of the white mutation in existence at present. The Recessive type was bred first in New Zealand and England simultaneously during 1908, although the latter mutation was lost. The German Dominant White appeared in the 1920's, and in this case a slight trace of lipochrome remains in the primary flight feathers, giving them a lemon appearance. The genetical difference between these two forms is explained later.

The complete absence of lipochrome can also occur independently of the melanin group. This gives rise to the so-called Blue canaries, which, as seen in the Lizard mutation of this type, are more grayish than blue. Capped birds thus have a white rather

Below: *Because of differences in the structure of the feather vane, canaries of yellow feather type appear more strongly, or intensively, colored.*

than yellow area on the top of the head. The accompanying table sums up the basic mutations of this type. A third ground color resulted from the breeding of Red Factor

Presence (+) or Absence (−) of Pigment Types in the Principal Color Varieties

Color	Lipochrome	Melanin	Eumelanin
Green	+	+	+
Yellow	+	−	−
White (Recessive)	−	−	−
Blue	−	+	+
Cinnamon (Gold Brown)	+	−	+
Fawn (Silver Brown)	−	−	+

Buff And Yellow

Below: *In color canaries, the buff type is called "nonintensive."*

Canaries, using a Red Siskin to produce this hybrid cross. They have an orange background color, resulting from the input of both yellow and red pigments. Various other modifications, such as the dilution of melanin, have led to other developments in the field of so-called New Color Canaries.

Buff And Yellow

These two terms can be misleading because, in this context, neither refers strictly to the color of the canary, but to a difference in feather type. There is a slight variation in color however, because the distribution of lipochrome in the feathers is not consistent. In a yellow canary, it extends evenly throughout the feathering, whereas in a buff it stops short of the margins. This gives the individual feathers whitish edges, so overall the buff canary is a paler color than the yellow.

The distinction is particularly obvious in Red Factors, with buffs appearing frosted, and can be generally seen most clearly around the neck, where the feathers are often denser, as well as smaller. In the case of clear Whites, it will be necessary to examine them in the hand at first to spot a difference, with yellows possessing tighter feathers.

The feather tissue itself is in fact altered slightly, with buffs having marginally softer and larger feathers than yellow. The vast majority of pairings should be buff × yellow, irrespective of either bird's sex, to keep a good feather texture. Persistent double-buffing, which is the pairing of two buff birds together, predisposes to feather cysts. The feathers, because of their size and softness, do not develop properly, giving rise to the condition known as 'lumps'.

Variegation: Definition And Forms

Variegation is said to occur in the feathering when the melanins do not extend uniformly over the body but are broken by light patches, which are variable in size and distribution. As a result, canaries are

Above: *The one bird is designated Clear, while the plumage of the other qualifies it as Lightly Variegated.*

often classified on grounds of their degree of variegation, especially for exhibition purposes.

In the case of Self canaries, there is no

Below: *Though Variegated birds are quite variably marked, certain areas of the plumage are likely to be dark: around the eyes, for example.*

Canaries described as Foul are generally deemed to have only one small patch of light feathering with a maximum size of 1.875 cm (¾ in) in diameter or up to three similarly colored feathers together in the tail or wings. The definition varies slightly according to the breed concerned, as does the term Ticked, which is effectively the 'clear' equivalent of 'fouled.' A minor area of dark plumage is allowed in this case, fulfilling similar criteria.

The term Variegated is reserved for birds which fit into none of the previous groupings. In instances where the majority of the plumage is light in color, the canaries are said to be Lightly Variegated, whereas if dark markings predominate, they are referred to as being Heavily Variegated.

variegation whatsoever in the plumage, including the flights and tail. The term is applied only to birds with some or all of the melanin pigments present, such as greens or blues. The reverse situation is seen in Clear individuals, which lack any melanins in their plumage.

Genetical Principles

Characteristics such as color or feather type are coded in the body by means of genes, located on paired structures

Below: *New Color canaries are the result of breeding various mutations into a single individual—here the ground color exhibits the red factor, while the melanins have been affected by dilute factors.* referred to as chromosomes, present in all animal cells. The means by which such characters emerge in the offspring was elucidated by Gregor Mendel, following his work with pea plants

during the late nineteenth century.

Considering just one pair of genes, coding for yellow or buff feathering in this instance, there are three effective combinations:

1. Yellow + Yellow.
2. Buff + Buff.
3. Yellow + Buff.

The first two combinations are known as homozygous, because the gene on each chromosome is identical, but in the third case, one gene corresponds to yellow and the other to buff. This bird would be referred to as heterozygous. Under such circumstances, one gene is likely to prove dominant to the other, which is hence recessive. The dominant gene shows itself in the bird's appearance, which will thus have yellow feathering, but genetically it is said to be, "split for" (represented by "/") buff. The genotype of a canary can thus vary from its phenotype.

Adopting symbols for the standard buff × yellow/buff pairing, it is possible to calculate the likely percentage of offspring of each type. The ratio will not necessarily prove accurate in every instance, as it is based on results from a large number of pairings:

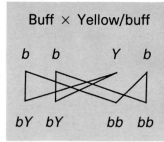

Buff × Yellow/buff

b b Y b

bY bY bb bb

It is possible to produce homozygous yellows by pairing two yellow/buff birds together.

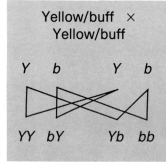

Yellow/buff × Yellow/buff

Y b Y b

YY bY Yb bb

Facing page: Intensive Red Factor cock. Since the flights are principally colored with melanins in the wild form of the canary, in clear birds they become white.

25% Yellow (YY); 50% Yellow/buff (Yb); 25% Buff (bb)—this gives the Mendelian ratio of 1 : 2 : 1. Such yellows are not popular with breeders however, because the quality of the feathering soon deteriorates when the canaries are paired together. The effect is most obvious in the case of the *Gibber italicus,* which is unique because it does not occur in the buff form. The plumage in this breed is now so degenerate that areas of the body such as the breastbone remain unfeathered.

Breeding Crests

The crested form of the canary is dominant to the plainhead and always paired with this type. The results expected are as shown above for the yellow/buff x buff pairing, because it is impossible to have homozygous crests. Such chicks are not viable, and fail to hatch or die very shortly afterwards because of a lethal factor in their genetic make-up. Plainheads can be mated together without the problem arising, but will not, of course, produce any crested offspring.

Breeding German Dominant Whites

A similar lethal factor is involved when Dominant Whites of any breed are paired together, so that one quarter of their potential offspring are non-viable. As a result

Above: *The* Gibber italicus, *a breed that exemplifies the extreme effects of the yellow feather type.*

therefore, heterozygous whites are mated with yellow ground canaries rather than each other, yielding chicks of each color in roughly equal proportions.

Breeding Cinnamons

The genes responsible for this color are confined to the sex chromosomes, which may be of a different length, being responsible for determining the canary's gender. Those of the cock are of an equal size known as XX, whereas in the case of a hen, there is a shorter Y chromosome, with the pair being represented as XY. Genes occurring on the lower part of the X chromosome must therefore be expressed, whether dominant or recessive, because there is no corresponding gene on the shorter Y chromosome to mask their effect. As a result, hens of a sex-linked mutation cannot be split for this color. A pairing involving a Green/Cinnamon cock and a Cinnamon hen is

Above: *The Gloster Fancy is a breed of canary that features the crest mutation.*

73

Breeding Cinnamons

diagrammed thus (the minus sign indicates no gene):

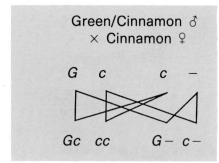

Green/Cinnamon ♂
× Cinnamon ♀

G c c $-$

Gc cc $G-$ $c-$

Expectations run as follows: 25% Green

Above: *Green canaries exhibit the same combination of lipochrome and melanin found in the wild canary.*

hens (G−); 25% Cinnamon hens (c−); 25% Cinnamon cocks (cc); 25% Green/Cinnamon cocks (Gc).

There are another five possible pairings involving these colors:
1. Green cock × Cinnamon hen ⟶ 50% Green/Cinnamon cocks + 50 % Green hens.
2. Cinnamon cock × Green hen ⟶ 50% Green/Cinnamon cocks + 50 % Cinnamon hens.
3. Cinnamon cock × Cinnamon hen ⟶ 100% Cinnamon cocks and hens.
4. Green/Cinnamon cock × Green hen ⟶ 25% Green cocks + 25% Green/Cinnamon cocks + 25 % Green hens + 25% Cinnamon hens.
5. Green cock × Green hen ⟶ 100% Green cocks and hens.

Unfortunately it is not possible to predict accurately the pattern of variegation which will result from a particular pairing, because simple dominant or recessive inheritance does not apply in this case.

Depictions of the ideal type, or conformation, that the Border canary should possess, here shown in two colors, Green and Cinnamon.

The Breeds And Exhibition Points

The first attempt to classify canaries into breeds was made by Hervieux, 'Inspector of Canary Breeding' to the Duchess of Berry. He included twenty-nine varieties in his book, *Traite des Serin de Canarie,* published in 1709. Some of these were merely established plumage variants present in the stock at that time rather than distinct types of canaries. Since this time, new breeds have been evolved, while some, such as the London Fancy, are now extinct. They are arranged here in alphabetical order for convenience.

American Singer

As its name suggests, this breed originated in America and is kept mainly for its song. American Singers have been bred from Roller and Border Fancy stock, with the former breed contributing sixty-nine per cent of the pedigree. The quest to establish the American Singer began in 1934, and

Above: *Winners in the American Singer Division of the 1981 National Cage Bird Show.*

subsequently in 1943, a club for the variety came into being.

STANDARD OF THE AMERICAN SINGER: The Freedom of Song—10

points. The Rendition of Song—60 points. Body Conformation (must not exceed 14.6 cm [5¾ in]—20 points. Overall Condition—10 points. Total: 100 points.

These canaries are judged primarily on their singing ability, with no points being awarded for color. The breed does have recognized characteristics however, and should perch at an angle between 35 and 45 per cent to the horizontal, as well as having a bold disposition. They are not common in Europe, but could be bred without too much difficulty, as foundation stock is available. It will take at least four years to produce American Singers however, from the initial pairings. Such birds are popular as pets because of the freedom with which they sing.

Belgian Fancy

The Belgian Fancy is one of the oldest surviving breeds and reached its peak of popularity during the last century. These birds were

Below: *The Belgian Fancy is a breed in which attention focuses on the shape and carriage of the bird.*

derived from Dutch Canaries, and, indeed, the larger coarse feathered strain developed here was known as the Dutch Belgian form. In Belgium itself, cities such as Brussels and Antwerp became centers for producing thinner, more slender birds referred to as French Belgians. Clear birds in particular were highly prized, while Belgian stock was also widely used in producing other breeds, now accepted as British, such as the Yorkshire.

77

Above: *Border canaries, a breed which many fanciers deem the most pleasing in form.*

Belgian Fancy Canaries had a reputation for being more delicate than other breeds however, and this may have contributed to their decline. In addition, considerable training was required to stage these birds adequately, and most strains were never prolific breeders.

Type and posture are the two main features of the Belgian Fancy Canaries. They are generally smaller today than formerly, when they reached a length of over 17.78 cm (7 in). This breed has a relatively small head, a long neck and body coupled with unusually high shoulders. The legs are also particularly long and upright, giving the bird a vertical stance, with the shoulders and tail in a straight line. In a good exhibition specimen, the neck should be extended with the head pointing downward during judging.

Border Fancy

Border Fancy Canaries were first bred in Scotland, where they were known simply as Common Canaries. A shoemaker is said to have been responsible for their introduction to England when he moved from Langholm to Cumberland. The breed was adopted as the Cumberland Canary, and the dispute over its name was not resolved until 1890, when the term Border Fancy was accepted, following a meeting at Hawick. Its origins have been lost, but the Border is certainly a composite breed, with Lizards, Rollers and even perhaps London Fancies contributing to its early development during the 1820's. Being one of the smaller breeds it was popularly known among fanciers as the 'Wee Gem', but in recent years the size of the Border Fancy has been increased somewhat, following the introduction of Norwich blood.

It is today one of the most popular varieties, being a reliable breeder and thus quite freely available, in colors which include green, yellow, white and cinnamon. Border Canaries make an ideal introduction to the hobby of canary keeping. A further advantage for some fanciers is that this breed is never color-fed for exhibition purposes, following a decision taken back in 1901 by the members of the Border Fancy Canary Club. These canaries do

Above: *In this Variegated Border, the dark areas are colored cinnamon.*

require more training than some other breeds however, as they should always be lively and alert, moving freely from perch to perch during judging. This can be achieved by gently moving the hand to and fro close to the perch, encouraging the canary to hop back and forth in the cage, from an early age.

Standard of the Border Fancy: Head: Small, round and neat looking; beak fine; eyes central to roundness of head and body—10 points. Body: Back well-filled and nicely rounded, running in almost a straight line from the gentle rise over the shoulders to the point of the tail; chest also nicely rounded, but

Above: *Eight-week-old Border canaries illustrate some of the color varieties possible in the breed.*

neither heavy nor prominent, the line gradually tapering to the vent—15 points. Wings: Compact and carried close to the body, just meeting at the tips, at a little lower than the root of the tail—10 points. Legs: Of medium length, showing little thigh, fine and in harmony with other points, yet corresponding—5 points. Plumage: Close, firm, fine in quality, presenting a smooth, glossy silken appearance, free from frill or roughness—10 points. Tail: Closely packed and narrow, being rounded and filled in at the root—5 points. Position: Semi-erect, standing at an angle of 60°; carriage gay, jaunty with full poise of the head—15 points. Color: Rich, soft and pure, as level in tint as possible throughout, but extreme depth and hardness such as color-feeding gives are debarred—15 points. Health: Condition and cleanliness shall have due weight—10 points. Size: Not to exceed 13.75 cm (5½ in) in length—5 points. Total: 100 points.

Above: *The Lancashire Coppy,* coppy *being another word for* crest.

Cinnamon Canary
This mutation, initially recognized as a distinct breed, was very popular at the beginning of the century. It was developed in the South of England to resemble the Norwich and is often included in the classification for this breed at shows today. Northern breeders aimed to produce Cinnamons closer to Yorkshire or Belgian type stock, and these were generally a lighter brown in color. Cinnamon Canaries are, not surprisingly, assessed largely on their color.

STANDARD OF THE CINNAMON CANARY: Color—35 points. Type and Shape—20 points. Quality of Feather—15 points. Wing Carriage and Tail—10 points. Size—10 points. Condition, Cleanliness, etc.—10 points. Total: 100 points.

Above: *Of all the canary breeds, the Crested is the most massive.*

Columbus Fancy

The Columbus Fancy is another American breed, developed initially in the State of Ohio, becoming centered on the city of Columbus. Border Fancies and Lancashire Coppies formed the basis of the bloodstock, although Norwich and Gloster Fancy Canaries were also used. It thus occurs in both crested and non-crested forms, with the crest normally black. The standards for the two types differ somewhat as shown:

STANDARD OF THE COLUMBUS FANCY— CRESTED: Crest: Size (half-dollar shape, droop, round rosette)— 45 points. Body—10 points. Condition—10 points. Beak—5 points. Feather—10 points. Position—10 points. Neck (fullness)—5 points. Legs (short, thighs well-feathered)—

5 points. Total: 100 points.

NON-CRESTED: Head: Large and well-rounded—25 points. Body: Stout, chubby, 13.75–15.00 cm (5½–6 in) in length—20 points. Eyebrows—10 points. Beak: Short, neat—10 points. Feather: 'Leafy' texture—10 points. Position (also size and shape)—15 points. Health and Cleanliness—10 points. Total: 100 points.

Above: *The Fife Fancy is here represented by a Cinnamon Self.*

Crested Canary

Although there are now various breeds of canary which have a crested form, it is the variety related to the Norwich which is still known independently as the Crested Canary. The crested mutation itself was known by 1793, before most of today's type breeds were established. Norwich breeders adopted it as a characteristic for their birds, so Crested and Plainhead forms were then produced.

The introduction of Lancashire Canaries in the search for a larger crest changed the appearance of the Crested Norwich, also increasing their size dramatically. The breed had an initial boom in popularity which fell as prices went out of the reach of most breeders. A more serious problem for the breed itself was the combined disabilities of blindness and feather 'lumps'. These cysts arise directly from breeding for soft or curled plumage, as is the case with a crest, because the feathers may curl over before penetrating through the skin surface, and so

Below: *A Clear Buff Plainhead of Norwich or Crested type.*

grow back into the feather follicle itself.

Crested Canaries have enjoyed a minor boost in popularity again during recent years. They should have a full even circular crest positioned centrally on the head, extending to the level of the eyes. The center must be small, while the feathers in the crest should be broad, and overall a weeping crest is preferred, as distinct from those with a flat appearance. These feathers may need to be trimmed slightly during the breeding season to give better visibility.

Internal drinkers or wider holes are necessary to protect the crest from damage during the remainder of the year, especially prior to the exhibition season. Color-feeding is not required for Crested Canaries however, unlike Norwich Fancy birds.

As explained in the genetics chapter, there is a lethal factor which prevents the development of homozygous crested chicks. As a result, all crested birds should be paired with non-crested stock, known as Crestbreds (the Plainhead form), produced from a previous pairing of Crested and Crestbred Canaries together. The crested mutation is itself a dominant character.

Dutch Canaries
The Dutch Canary in its original form has been lost, being one of the oldest varieties described two hundred years ago. It may have been the first frilled variety, from which today's related breeds,

including the Dutch Frill, are descended. Dutch Canaries also contributed to other 'type' varieties, including Scotch Fancies, Yorkshire and Lancashire Canaries.

Fife Fancy
The Fife Fancy is a recent addition to the established type breeds, and arose from the desire of Border fanciers to re-establish a small breed following the gradual increase in size which had occurred in their 'Wee Gem'. At a meeting which took place at Kirkcaldy, Scotland during 1957, the maximum size for the new breed was fixed at 10.63 cm (4¼ in), a full 2.5 cm (1 in) smaller than the current Border standard. The points awarded for both breeds are virtually the same however, but 20 points are available for size in the case of the Fife Fancy.

This breed received a considerable boost back in 1973, when W. and D. Lumsden won the top Canary award at the English National Exhibition with a Fife Fancy. Since then, these canaries have become increasingly popular.

Frilled Canaries
Frilled canaries are more popular in mainland Europe than in Britain and the United States. Three main types are recognized, although the basic frill pattern is the same for each, with additional frills

Above: *Frilled canaries are characterized by contour feathers that curl as they grow.*

distinguishing the various varieties.

Their curled feathering can be divided into three major parts. The Mantle runs down the back, divided by a central line, with the frills curling over the shoulders. The Jabot, also known as the claw or waistcoat, is formed by the breast feathers which should curve inward to form a closed shell in the center. The Fins occur at the top of the thighs and extend upward, curling over the wings. In addition to this basic pattern, there are specific requirements for each particular breed.

The Parisian Frill is probably most common in Britain and used to reach a length of 20.6 cm (81/4 in), but today 17.5 cm (7 in) is about the upper limit for size. An unusual requirement for this bird is that its nails should be rounded in the shape of a corkscrew. The Paduan Frill resembles the Parisian form but is also crested.

The Dutch Frill is generally smaller than its French counterpart, but these two varieties were often inter-bred so pure Dutch stock is not always easily obtainable. The Southern Dutch form has given rise to the *Gibber italicus* or Italian Humpback Frill, known only as a yellow rather than buff feather type. It has no

Above: *A group of Gloster Coronas, members of a breed favored for its liveliness.*

feathering on the breastbone or thighs.

One of the newest type breed, derived from the *Gibber italicus,* is the *Giboso espanol* which was first exhibited at the C.O.M. World show held in Belgium early during 1982. These canaries originated in Spain and apparently possess an

extra cervical vertebra which gives them an even more elongated neck. The standard for the *Giboso espanol* calls for an angle of 45°

between the body and tail when the bird is perched.

Other Frills are also recognized, with another recent addition being a Miniature Japanese variety bred in a Red Factor form. Frilled canaries are not perhaps birds for the beginner and certainly do not appeal to all breeders, but there are no additional significant problems in their management. Perhaps surprisingly, in spite of their curled plumage they do not appear to be troubled by feather cysts as much as other breeds.

Gloster Fancy
The Gloster Fancy Canary was developed initially during the 1920's by Mrs. Rogerson, who lived in Gloucestershire and bred the first crested examples of this type, working in conjunction with J. McLay and A.W. Smith. These canaries arose from crossings between small Border Fancies and Crested Rollers. Progress was initially slow, with only thirty

being exhibited at the 1940 National Exhibition, but since the Second World War Glosters have become one of the most popular canaries with 961 on show forty years later.

Their dainty appearance and lively disposition were in contrast to the existing Crested Canaries. The crest was much more compact than that of the established varieties and did not obscure the eyes. The crested form in the case of a Gloster is known as the Corona, whereas the plainhead equivalent is referred to as the Consort. Pairs should again consist of one bird of each type, irrespective of sex, because of the lethal factor which becomes apparent when two crested birds are mated together. Buff Glosters are much more common than yellows and partly as a result of these continued buff to buff pairings, feather cysts are becoming an increasing problem in this breed.

Apart from this drawback, Glosters have much in their favor for the newcomer to the Canary Fancy. They are available at moderate prices and generally breed well, being reliable parents. For exhibition purposes they do not require color-feeding, and compared to the Border, are relatively easy to train, having first been accustomed to a show cage shortly after weaning. The

Below: *In the Gloster Fancy, a noncrested bird, or plainhead, is known as a Consort.*

competition is often fierce however, and gently brushing the crest with a damp tooth-brush will help to improve the Corona's appearance.

STANDARD OF THE GLOSTER FANCY—CONSORT: Head broad and round at every point, with good rise over center of skull—15 points. Eyebrow heavy, showing brow—5 points. CORONA: Neatness: regular, unbroken round shape, eye discernible—15 points; with definite center—5 points. Body: Back well filled and wings lying closely thereto; full neck, chest nicely rounded without prominence—20 points. Tail: Closely folded and well-carried—5 points. Plumage: Close, firm, giving a clear-cut appearance; of good quality and natural color—15 points. Carriage: Alert, with quick, lively movement–10 points. Legs & Feet: Medium length, without blemish—5 points. Size: For tendency to the diminutive—15 points. Condition: Health and cleanliness—10 points. Total: 100 points.

Lancashire Canary
The direct line of Lancashire Canaries was lost to the Canary Fancy during the Second World War. In recent years however, the Old Varieties Canary Association (O.V.C.A.) of Great Britain has been instrumental in trying to recreate this breed using Crested and Norwich Fancy blood, which the Lancashire

Above: *The Lancashire Canary was developed in an era when large size was emphasized.*

helped to create during the last century. Yorkshire Fancy Canaries also have a part to play in this quest. Lancashire Canaries could reach a length of 19.4 cm (7 ¾ in) and size was an important characteristic of these birds. They were especially popular in their home county, with the crested form, known as the Coppy, being highly prized in the Manchester area, giving rise to their alternative name Manchester Coppies. Variegated stock was unknown, and clears reigned supreme, with Green birds bred in Holland finding favor in Britain.

Writers of that period stated that Lancashire Canaries did not reproduce well, and this was almost certainly a major reason for their loss. Foster parents often had to be used, and it was recommended for maximum size that no pair reared more than two chicks at a time. Good hens fetched a premium and were also sought-after for pairing with Linnets to produce mules.

A Clear-cap Gold Lizard cock—Gold and Silver refer to the yellow and buff feather types.

Lizard Canary

The Lizard, with its pattern of distinctive markings resembling those of the reptile's scales, cannot be confused with any other breed of canary. It was included by Hervieux in his original list of varieties back in 1709 and has remained almost unchanged down to the present day, being bred exclusively for its markings rather than its shape.

The dark spangles on the plumage are the main show point for the breed, but the head feathering is also significant and known as the Cap. A Clear-cap has an oval area of plumage with no dark feathers extending from the top of the beak to the back of the head. If the clear area extends to the sides of the face, this is a serious fault, referred to as Bald-faced, while any extension down the neck is likewise penalized.

Until the middle of the 1870's, only Lizards with clear caps could be exhibited. The cap can also be split into two

Below: *The light edging of the buff-type feathers is nicely apparent on this Silver Lizard.*

however, when the canary is referred to as Broken-capped, and these birds are generally paired with Clear-caps, to prevent excess capping appearing in the stock. It is also possible to obtain Lizards without caps, and these are called Non-caps.

The spangles must be in regular lines running down the back, gradually increasing in size. They should be crescent-shaped, giving rise to the old northern term for these birds, which was "mooned 'uns". Similar markings on the breast are described as 'rowings'. The buff form of the Lizard is known as the Silver, being paler than the yellow feather type referred to as the Gold.

In recent years, the number of Lizards has risen encouragingly following their supposed decline during the Second World War, although forty-five were benched at the 1945 National Exhibition. They are generally reliable breeders and are also free from the problem of feather cysts. For exhibition purposes, an unflighted bird having molted once to obtain its spangled appearance while retaining its nest flight and tail feathers shows to best advantage. Feather-plucking will seriously mar their chances however, and great care should be taken when the birds are molting. Color-feeding is also necessary at this time.

STANDARD OF THE LIZARD CANARY: Spangles: For regularity and distinctness—25 points. Feather Quality: For tightness and silkiness—15 points. Ground Color: For depth and evenness—10 points. Breast: For extent and regularity of rowings—10 points. Wings and Tail: For neatness and darkness—10 points. Cap: For neatness and shape—10 points. Covert Feathers: For darkness and lacing—5 points. Eyelash: For regularity and clarity—5 points. Beak, Legs and

Above: *A white ground color produces a variety of Lizard canary called Blue.*

Feet: For darkness—5
points. Steadiness and
Staging: Length should
not exceed 13.1 cm (5¼
in)—5 points. Total: 100
points.

London Fancy

These canaries were
popular during the last
century, but their
numbers were declining
by late Victorian times,
and all trace of the
breed finally
disappeared during the
1930's. Even in 1923,
C.A. House in his book
Canaries conceded, "It
is with regret that I write
of the handsome variety
as a relic of bygone
days, for there are very
few left in the land."

Much discussion has
since been generated
among fanciers over the
breed's origins and loss.
Young London Fancy
canaries resembled
Lizards in nest feather,
and it is likely that there
was a close relationship
between the two breeds.
The reported breeding
of a London Fancy from
a pair of Lizards in the
1880's was never
confirmed however, and
probably inaccurate.
During 1978, the
similarity between the
breeds was further
questioned, somewhat
contrary to current
views, in the August
10th issue of the British
periodical *Cage and
Aviary Birds*, by Mr. H.
Roberson, then in his
eighties. He knew
breeders of the original
London Fancy prior to
the First World War and
claimed they did not
recognize this apparent
affinity.

Attempts to save the
breed by using Clear
Borders and Norwich
Fancy stock merely

Above: *The dark flights
were a prominent feature
of the London Fancy
canary.*

speeded its demise. Illustrations and contemporary descriptions show the London Fancy as being a deep yellow color with blackish flights and tail. Other forms, known as Spangle-backs, were also recorded. The Buff type was referred to as the Mealy, while the term for the yellow feathered variety was Jonque, which is perhaps less confusing for the novice than the descriptions in use today.

Above: *As new feathers grow in, the effect of color feeding is apparent.*

Malinois

Malinois were bred initially from Roller stock and developed for their distinctive song largely in Belgium. They are still relatively unknown outside the continental mainland.

New Color (Color-Bred) Canaries

All these varieties have been bred during the twentieth century, although some may have been known and lost prior to this date. The first mutant reported in 1900 from Holland was named

Agate, as its grayish appearance matched a description of a variety reported by Hervieux nearly two centuries earlier. The Agate is known in Britain as the Dilute, this being a more accurate term because of the reduction of melanin in the plumage. In many cases unfortunately, there is still no unification of

from another species. Experimental crossings with the South American Black-hooded Red Siskin *(Spinus cucullatus)* yielded fertile cock hybrids which were referred to as F_1 Copper Hybrids. It soon became apparent however that the Siskin's red coloration was produced by not just one gene but several, making the problem of transference much more complex.

The color of Red Factor Canaries today is still at best reddish-orange. Pairings usually involve a bird of each feather type, as for other breeds, but the terms 'yellow' and 'buff' are replaced by others including 'red orange' and 'apricot', and 'non-frosted' and 'frosted' respectively. The latter description was coined from the whitish ends of the canary's feathers, which gave it a frosted appearance.

Following a decision taken by the Canary Color Breeders' Association, color-feeding is now permitted following an earlier ruling made in 1947

nomenclature, so dual systems operate on the continent and in Britain. When the agate mutation was introduced to brown stock, Isabels (or Cinnamons) were bred.

The most popular New Colored variety today is the Red Factor, which is in fact a hybrid bird. It was developed as a result of the work of the German geneticist Dr. Duncker, who in 1929 proposed that it would be possible to breed Red Canaries by introducing the red gene which forbade it. Apart from the coloring agent itself, the diet just prior to and during the molt is also significant in producing a good color in Red Factors. Lutein, which will give the plumage a yellow tint must be reduced at this time. Rich sources of lutein include greenfood and seeds such as rape and hemp and egg yolk. As a result, these foods are withheld, and a basic diet for molting Red Factors often consists of groats (hulled oats) and niger, supplemented with grated carrot and soft food which does not contain any egg yolk.

The color of these canaries only shows to best advantage in natural light, and indoors, at many exhibitions, their coloration may not be as bright as when they are seen in aviaries. Following excessive breeding for color, the type of these canaries was beginning to decline, and so the standard was altered during 1973 in an attempt to overcome this problem, thus giving a maximum of 30 points in total for five features.

STANDARD OF NEW COLOR CANARIES: Maximum length 12.5 cm (5 in). Color—55 points. Body Outline—10 points. Head—5 points. Neck— 5 points. Wings—5 points. Legs and Feet— 2 points. Tail—3 points. Plumage—5 points. Condition—5 points. Staging—5 points. Total: 100 points.

Over fifty varieties of New Color Canaries are now recognized. It is an exciting area for the

Above: *Orange and Cinnamon canaries.*

breeder who is interested in genetics, with further new additions to the established list likely to occur in the future.

Norwich Fancy

The Norwich Plainhead was developed initially around the East Anglian city bearing its name. The original stock was probably brought from the continent, perhaps by Flemish weavers towards the end of the seventeenth century. The Norwich became transformed as a breed during the late nineteenth century, with a noticeable increase in size following crossings with Lancashire Canaries, which took place at first in the North of England. The increased emphasis on 'type' probably arose directly as a result of the introduction of color-feeding in this breed, which thus reduced the significance of breeding for natural color.

Norwich Plainheads are now known popularly as the John Bulls of the Canary Fancy because of their

Below: The Norwich Plainhead is one of the stockiest of the type-canary breeds.

stocky appearance. A further trend to increasing size during the 1920's resulted in buff to buff pairings, leading to thicker-feathered birds and the problem of feather lumps, which can still be a major handicap to breeders today. Norwich Canaries are not considered to be a prolific breed, and foster pairs of other varieties are sometimes used to rear their chicks. Good stock is relatively expensive, and so the newcomer is probably best advised to gain experience with another, experience with another, more reliable breed before progressing to keeping Norwich.

STANDARD OF THE NORWICH FANCY: Type: Short and cobby. Back broad and well filled in, showing a slight rise transversely. Chest broad and deep, giving an expansive curved front and sweeping from under therefrom in one full curve to the tail.

Ideal length 15.0–15.6 cm (6–6¼ in). Stance a position at about an angle of 45°—25 points. Head: Proportionately bold and assertive in its carriage. A full forehead rising from a short neat beak. To be well rounded over and across the skull. Cheeks full and clean featured; eye to be well-placed and unobscured—10 points. Neck: Short and

Above: *A pair of Variegated Norwich canaries.*

thick, continuing to run from the back skull on to the shoulders and from a full throat into the breast—10 points. Wings: Short and well-braced, meeting nicely at the tips to rest lightly, yet closely on the rump—10 points. Tail: Short, closely-packed and well filled in at the root. Rigidly carried, giving an all of one appearance with the body—5 points. Legs & Feet: Well set back. Feet perfect—5 points. Condition: In full bloom of perfect health. Bold and bouncing in movement—10 points. Quality of Feather: Close and fine in texture, presenting the smooth, silky plumage necessary to give a clean-cut contour—10 points. Color: Rich, bright and level throughout, with clean sheen or brilliancy. Yellows a deep orange. Buffs rich in ground color and well-mealed— 10 points. Staging: Clean and correctly staged—5 points. Total: 100 points.

Roller Canaries

The Roller Canary has been popular for centuries by virtue of its song. Rollers originated in Germany, especially in the Harz Mountain region, early during the

Below: *Unlike this ordinary canary, good Rollers keep their beaks closed while singing, which makes the sound softer and more mellifluous.*

Canary's domestication so that Blangrove, writing in 1675, stated that the "German birds in handsomeness and song excel those brought from the Canaries."

Rollers will of course sing naturally, and their name is derived from their manner of delivery. For competition purposes though, training is essential and revolves around the ability of the bird to reproduce distinct musical passages, known as 'tours' and 'rolls'. There are thirteen

Above: *The Yorkshire canary, prized for its upright carriage.*

recognized in British competitions, some of which retain their original German names, while others are translated, but only a very small handful of Rollers can sing them all.

Training used to be accomplished exclusively by means of a tutor or 'Schoolmaster' bird, with the young cocks being kept in small cages close at hand, learning to mimic the older canary. A close watch should be maintained at this stage to remove any youngsters which show faults in their repertoire, as they may also be copied by their fellows. Tapes are now popular as training aids and records were used in the past, although a good 'schoolmaster' remains preferable.

Competition Rollers must be close-ringed with coded rings issued by Roller Canary societies while they are still in the nest. The birds are exhibited in darkened cages and should start singing once the judge removes the cover from the front, letting in light. The song of such Rollers may range nearly three octaves, and perhaps not surprisingly these canaries appeal especially to those with a good musical ear. Untrained birds in a garden aviary or kept as pets will also bring much pleasure to their owners and generally breed freely.

STANDARD OF THE ROLLER CANARY: Hollow Roll—10 points. Bass—10 points. Water Glucke—10 points. Glucke—10 points. Glucke Roll—10 points. Hollow Bell—8 points. Schockel—8 points. Flutes—6 points. Water Roll—6 points. Deep Bubbling Water Tour—5 points. Bell Roll—3 points. Bell Tour—2 points. General Effect—10 points. Total: 98 points. *N.B.* Various deductions can also be made for faults.

Scotch Fancy

On account of its unusual shape, the Scotch Fancy is sometimes known as the Bird O'Circle. These canaries were developed around Glasgow at first from Belgian stock during the 1830's, being christened here as Dons. They then became generally popular throughout Scotland, so that entries close to a thousand individuals could be expected at major shows during the 1870's.

Subsequent repeated crossings between Scotch and Belgian Fancy birds caused great harm to both varieties and led to their decline. They were also reputed to be poor breeders, unlike most of today's stock. Scotch Fancy Canaries have been revived successfully in recent years, again mainly through the efforts of the O.V.C.A., with a standard for the breed being established in 1971. These birds

Above: Yorkshire canary in a show cage.

should be of lively disposition and have a good action or 'travelling' on the show bench, hopping readily from perch to perch and adopting their characteristic stance for the judge's benefit.

A miniature form of the Scotch Fancy, known as Japanese Hoso, was first exhibited at the National Exhibition in 1977. It has not proved popular with fanciers however, and so is unlikely to become widely known.

STANDARD OF THE SCOTCH FANCY: Shape: Body long, tapering and curved in the form of a half circle, convex above, concave below, with a clean outline, feather being close, short and tight—20 points. Head and neck: Small, neat, snaky head. Long tapering neck—10 points. Shoulders and Back: High, narrow, rounded shoulders, well-filled in. Long, narrow, well-filled back curving from shoulders to tail—20 points. Tail: Long, narrow, closely folded and well-curved under the perch—5 points. Style, Nerve and Travelling: Well raised up, forming a high circle. Bold, free and jaunty carriage with plenty of life and action—25 points. Size: Approximately 16.88 cm (6¾ in.)—10 points. Quality and Condition: Clean, healthy, perfect condition—10 points. Total: 100 points.

Spanish Timbrado
These canaries are named in part after their country of origin, being first recognized as a separate breed in 1962. They are said to have arisen from crossings between local canaries and wild stock, with their

Above: *According to the standard, the beak of a Yorkshire should be "neat and fine."*

appearance being greenish-gray as a rule, and averaging 12.50—13.75 cm (5–5½ in) in length.

Timbrados are popular for their song, and this part of their name arises from the word 'timbre' which describes their metallic ringing notes. A song standard has been established for the breed, comprised largely of Bell Tours, Connective Tours, and passages of 'Castanet' notes (which sound similar to the instrument which accompanies folk-dancing in the area), and the metallic notes. Embellishments are also recognized, with notes resembling the Glucke Roll of the Roller. The total number of points available for the judges is now 96, following a recent revision to the standard during 1979. Many of these canaries are bred locally on balconies in all-wire cages in the southern part of the country.

Yorkshire Canary

Yorkshire Canaries have undergone a noticeable

Below: *The fullness of the feathering on the neck and head is a point of considerable variability among Yorkshires.*

change in appearance since the days of the 1860's when they were first described. At this time, the ideal was jokingly considered slim enough to pass through a wedding ring. The Yorkshire has now lost its original slight stature but retained its length, and is still referred to as 'The Gentleman of the Fancy'. Crossings with Lancashire Canaries

Yorkshire Canary

Below: *A Yorkshire and a Norwich differ considerably in type.*

gave the Yorkshire size, while Norwich Fancy birds contributed color and improved the feather texture. Belgian stock was used to lend posture to the emerging breed.

Yorkshire Canaries are not easy birds to exhibit successfully and require color-feeding, although an individual with good natural color will still have an inherent advantage. Considerable time must be spent on training,

which can begin shortly after weaning. The youngsters should be accustomed to the show cage and perch steadily when confronted with a judging stick which, in this case, need only be a length of dowelling. Some breeders set the perches and nest pans relatively low in the cage so, right from the outset, there is no tendency for the birds to stoop down. It is vital that a good exhibition Yorkshire sits erect in the show cage, as position counts for 25 points.

The practice of pulling out tail feathers from unflighted stock so they regrow slightly longer may permanently mutilate the bird and is not recommended. Furthermore, with color feeding this unnatural 'growth' is obvious to all. In addition to the official standard, there are various markings which may indicate the class in which an individual should be entered at a show.

STANDARD OF THE YORKSHIRE CANARY: Head: Full, round and cleanly defined. Back skull deep and carried back in line with rise of shoulders. Eye as near center of head as possible. Shoulders proportionately broad, rounded and carried well up to and gradually merging into the head. Breast full and deep, corresponding to width and rise of shoulders and carried up full to base of beak which should be neat and fine—20 points. Body: Well rounded and gradually tapering throughout to tail—10 points. Position: Attitude erect with fearless carriage, legs long without being stilty, and slight lift behind—25 points. Feather— Close, short and tight. Wings proportionately long and evenly carried down the center of the back and firmly set on a compact and closely folded tail— 25 points. Size: Length approximately 16.9 cm (6¾ in.) with corresponding symmetrical proportions—10 points. Condition: Health, cleanliness and sound feathers, color pure and level—10 points. Total: 100 points.

Below: *Judging in progress at a Yorkshire Canary Club show in England.*

Health Problems

Canaries are not difficult birds to maintain in good health, providing their housing and feeding needs are never neglected. Certain specific problems, such as feather cysts, are more commonly associated with some breeds than others, but providing healthy stock is obtained in the first instance, then this need not detract from these varieties.

advice. This should be sought without delay so that treatment, where applicable, can start immediately and thus has a maximal chance of being effective.

Most sick canaries appear slightly fluffed up initially and may lose their appetite. Subsequently, they spend most of their time perched in one place and are dull and lethargic. Canaries when

In many cases of illness, the symptoms are far from specific, and distinguishing between the various possible causes will require veterinary

Above: *Anytime a canary is caught up offers an opportunity to examine the bird for illness.*

resting normally perch with just one foot gripping the perch, whereas those off-color often use both feet to maintain their balance.

Having removed a sick bird from the aviary, it will then benefit from being kept warm in a temperature of about 30° C (85° F). A hospital cage with an adjustable thermostatic control is a useful investment and enables the temperature to be reduced gradually as the patient recovers.

Accidents

Much can be done to prevent the risk of accidental injuries by ensuring there are no exposed ends of wire in the aviary and that the canaries are kept separate from other birds such as budgerigars, which are potentially dangerous companions. Resulting injuries fall into two main categories, those which involve bleeding and those leading to fractures.

Cuts Cuts on the feet and legs usually stop bleeding without

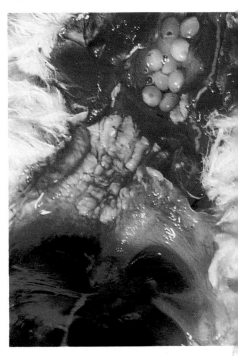

Above: *Grayish yellow deposits in the alimentary tract, caused by a fungus,* Candida albicans.

treatment, but a styptic pencil or a cold solution of potash alum can be used if necessary. Dressing such wounds is to be avoided if possible because it often causes the bird more distress. Smearing the injury with a safe antiseptic ointment should ensure that infecton does not then occur.

Fractures Fractures of

the leg are most common in the vicinity of the tarsometatarsus, extending below the knee joint, in the case of the canary. This bone is much longer than in other species such as the budgerigar and so is more exposed to injury. Careless handling and overgrown claws in particular can result in fractures, as the canary may get caught up and struggle fiercely. If a broken limb is suspected, then a veterinarian should be consulted and may splint the fracture. The chances of successful treatment depend on various factors, including the location and type of fracture as well as the age of the bird.

Bone is constantly undergoing simultaneous breakdown and replacement in the body, but during the molt it appears that the former process predominates, and so fractures are more likely to occur at this time. A readily available supply of cuttlefish bone should help to prevent any deficiency of calcium which is the major component of the skeletal system.

Breathing Problems
The description 'asthma' is often applied to all breathing disorders encountered in birds, but this is a much wider and somewhat incorrect usage of a specific human term. The respiratory system in birds differs from that of mammals because as well as the lungs, there is a series of air sacs which form a vital part. If the sacs become damaged, air can escape into the tissues, giving rise to swellings under the skin known as subcutaneous emphysema.

A canary with breathing difficulties may show pronounced, irregular tail movements associated with wheezing or gasping. This can be most noticeable when the birds have gone to roost at night and there is little background noise to mask these sounds. In some cases,

Above: *Budgies and canaries should not be housed together, for it is likely that the canary will be injured sooner or later.*

depending on the cause, a bird may survive for months with such a condition but is liable to die if stressed. Growths pressing on part of the respiratory system and air-sac mites can often be implicated in such instances.

More acute cases show marked signs of a general illness and may have a discharge from the eyes for example. Bacterial or viral infections are often responsible, and pox virus is considered separately later. An antibiotic to be given in the water or medicated seed may be prescribed by a veterinarian to combat bacterial infections. If more than one individual in a group is showing similar symptoms, it is probably worth having tests carried out to isolate the underlying cause as soon as possible. Management is again important in preventing such problems, and feeding moldy seed in particular should be avoided at all costs, because this can lead to fungal infections of the airways which are difficult to treat successfully.

Breeding Problems

One of the most common disorders affecting hen canaries, often at the start of the breeding season, is egg-binding, when the egg is retained in the oviduct and as a result cannot be laid successfully. Although several factors may be involved, low temperatures and a deficiency of calcium appear to predispose to this condition.

Affected birds appear distressed and perch unsteadily with their wings and tail hanging at an unusual angle. A hen may be found on the floor of a breeding cage, having appeared quite normal several hours beforehand. Rapid action is required to save an egg-bound bird, but transferred to a warm environment such as a hospital cage, the hen may lay the egg without further assistance. The vent region is often swollen, and the egg may be felt within, but gentle handling is required at all stages because if the egg breaks inside the body death is very likely to occur from subsequent infection.

It is useful to apply a little olive oil directly to the vent, which will act

Above: *Molds can produce lesions in the air sacs and lungs.*

as a lubricant and so assist the expulsion of the egg. Such eggs can be removed manually by careful manipulation, but this should not be undertaken lightly. If the canary does not improve after several hours in the warm cage then a veterinarian should be consulted for further advice. It is not advisable to breed with a hen which has been egg-bound until the next season at the earliest.

In some cases after egg-binding a protrusion is visible from the vent. This is part of the oviduct which has prolapsed because of the muscular exertion applied to free the egg. The tissue must be washed off with tepid water if it is dirty and smeared with an antiseptic ointment before being gently pushed back inside the vent. Repeated prolapses occur occasionally, and a temporary stitch inserted by a veterinarian is the only solution under these circumstances.

After the chicks have

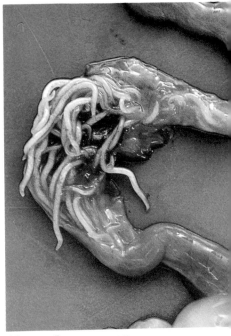

Above: *Severe worm infestation of the gut.*

hatched, hens sometimes develop moist, stained plumage on the breast. Before the cause was realized, it was assumed that the hen was sweating, but in fact this is a sign that the chicks have diarrhea. The hen's plumage becomes soiled as she broods her youngsters. As indicated under digestive problems, there are many possible causes of diarrhea, but in this case particularly, a check should be made to ensure that the rearing food has not been changed suddenly, or left to become sour.

Claw, Feet And Leg Problems:
Slipped Claw A
significant problem affecting young canaries, usually after weaning, is the condition known as slipped claw, when the back toe slips forward under the three front digits. This results in the bird being unable to perch properly, as it cannot grip with the affected foot, and also ruins it for exhibition purposes.

breeders often house young stock in cages with natural perches of a relatively thin diameter. A Vitamin B deficiency may also be involved, so supplementation, as indicated earlier, is useful. In addition, injuries leading to nerve damage may underlie perching problems of this nature, paralyzing the extensor muscle responsible for expanding the toe.

If a young canary develops 'slipped claw', then it may be possible to correct the defect by fixing the toe with an adhesive tape or plaster

The cause is not clear, but many feel that dowel perches of a regular diameter may be a contributing factor. To reduce the risk of 'slipped claw' therefore,

Above: *The foot of this canary is dead of dry gangrene that set in after an injury.*

up against the back of the leg for about ten days. Tying with cord or cotton is not recommended because the bird is more likely to get caught up in its cage, and this may lead to further damage. Furthermore, if the digit is tied back too tightly, the blood supply to the foot will be interfered with, leading perhaps to the loss of the toe.

Overgrown Claws

Overgrown claws can also result in injury, and eggs may be punctured when the hens are sitting. A regular check should be made to ensure that the claws do not become too long. Trimming is a fairly simple process when carried out in good light using a sharp pair of scissors or preferably bone clippers. The blood supply to the claw can be seen as a thin red line running a certain distance down each nail. The cut should be made a short way further down the claw, after the blood vessels have disappeared, so there is no risk of bleeding.

Below: *Overgrown claws occur more frequently as a bird ages and its activity declines.*

Scaly Leg In old canaries, the scales on the leg often become particularly prominent, and may be associated with varicose veins. There is also, however, a disease known as scaly leg, caused by a *Knemidocoptes* mite, which results in a progressive thickening around the feet. For this reason, the complaint is also called 'tassle foot'

113

because of the appearance of the affected digits. The mite responsible is related, if not identical, to that causing 'Scaly face' in budgerigars and can be killed by the lotions or creams marketed for this condition. Washing the perches off using a safe disinfectant solution may destroy any mites present there. Injuries to the feet are otherwise liable to predispose to infection by these parasites.

Digestive Problems

A number of bacterial infections result in digestive disorders manifested by abnormal, often greenish droppings. The canary itself will be off-color and fluffed up. In severe cases blood may be present in the droppings, but this should not be confused with the reddish color achieved by excess color-feeding, when the bird otherwise appears normal.

Cleanliness will reduce the risk of such infections to a minimum. As mentioned earlier, stale rearing foods and seed fouled by rodents are especially hazardous. Any canary with a suspected digestive disorder should be removed from its companions in case the complaint is

Below: *Varicose veins in the leg of a canary.*

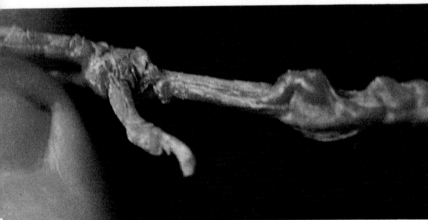

contagious. An antibiotic can often restore the bird to health, providing treatment begins as soon as possible and the instructions for its usage are followed implicitly. Underdosing or overdosing as well as continuing medication longer than indicated are all equally hazardous for various reasons. Other possible causes of digestive disorders, including viral infections and poisoning, are not likely to be cured by antibiotic treatment.

Eye Problems

An eye ailment is likely to be initially evident by reddening and discharge from the affected eye, followed by swelling and closure in most cases. If both eyes are involved, this could be a symptom of a much more serious generalized complaint such as pox.

Providing the canary appears alert and bright however, with only one eye closed, it is likely that a local irritation, perhaps initiated by a scratch, has set off the inflammation. Treatment with an

Below: *"Tassle foot" well describes* Knemidocoptes *mite infestation of the foot.*

antibiotic ophthalmic preparation applied several times daily is usually effective in overcoming any infection which may be present as a result of the injury. The canary should be restrained for a few seconds after treatment so that the drug can dissolve into the eye fluid and does not finish up simply wiped off on to a perch.

Feather Problems: Baldness A partial loss of feathering leading to

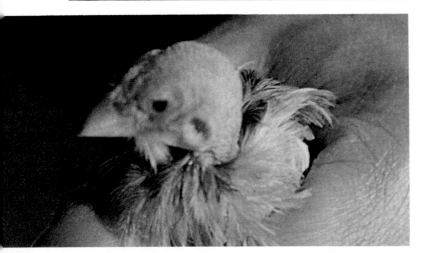

Above: *Canary with alopecia (baldness) of the head; in this case the cause was never determined.*

localized areas of baldness is not uncommon in adult canaries, especially during the latter part of the breeding season. It has been suggested that the problem occurs more widely during wet years, particularly in German Rollers of the Green variety. A nutritional deficiency is likely to be involved, and so the addition of a tonic to the diet is recommended. The plumage is generally regrown at the next molt. In addition,

parasites such as lice and mites can cause irritation, feather damage and even loss if the bird is driven to pluck its feathers, so using an aerosol spray which kills such pests may also be useful.

Feather Cysts Feather cysts are most commonly seen in Norwich Fancy and Crested Canaries. They occur as a result of a feather curling back within its follicle during development rather than passing out through the skin as normal. These cysts, often called 'lumps' in the Fancy, vary in size depending partly on the number of neighboring follicles involved and

Above: *On this Norwich canary, the large feather cyst can be seen beneath the feathers in the region of the wing.*

also on the amount of internal debris which accumulates in them. A common site for such 'lumps' is on the wings, and they eventually rupture on to the skin surface, discharging their 'cheesy' contents, which then hardens.

Such cysts, known technically as *hypopteronosis cystica,* result from an inherited condition, and birds so affected should not be used for breeding purposes. These hens are sometimes crossed with British finches, to produce mules however, as the condition does not then show itself and the offspring themselves are infertile. There is no really satisfactory treatment leading to a cure, as it is an inherent weakness present in the feathering itself. Some success has been claimed using a thyroid gland extract in mild cases. The new feathering which results is paler than usual after treatment however, and recurrences often appear.

Parasitic Problems
There is a wide range of parasites to which canaries may be susceptible, and some have been mentioned earlier. Ecto-parasites are, however, now quite simple to control, irrespective of the type concerned. Northern Mite *(Ornithonyssus sylviarum)* spends the whole of its life on the bird, and using a safe aerosol to destroy such parasites will rapidly overcome the infection.

Above: *Liveliness and alertness are signs of health in canaries as well as many other bird species.*

Red Mite Red mite *(Dermanyssus gallinae)* only feeds for a short time on the bird before retreating back to dark crevices where it hides and breeds. Its eggs can hatch in only two days, and the complete life cycle passing through larval and nymphal stages to the adult may take only a week, and so a population explosion of these parasites can occur in a very short space of time. They feed on blood, which gives them their characteristic color, and young canaries in particular may become anemic as a result. Regular spraying will, however, kill any mites but must be linked with a thorough washing of the birds' surroundings using a suitable preparaton. Red Mite can survive in small numbers, without feeding, from one breeding season to the next, so all cages should also be washed as a precaution.

An additional hazard of Red Mite is that they can, by virtue of their feeding habits, transmit a blood parasite, *Lankesterella* to canaries. This localizes in the lymphocytes and monocytes of the white blood group and may underlie cases of nestling deaths. In adult canaries, infection is relatively inconspicuous. Another protozoa, *Isospora,* can cause diarrhea and wasting, leading to eventual death. With the disease itself being known as Coccidiosis, infection in this case results from ingestion of the oocyst stage, which then develops in the gut and invades the body. It is one possible cause of birds 'going light', which merely describes their weight loss. All these parasites occur in sparrows and spread to canaries can result from such wild birds.

Chewing Lice Chewing lice belonging to the

Below: *The Red Mite is a parasite that can be controlled quite readily.*

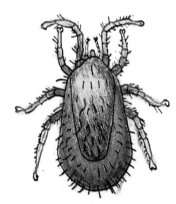

order Mallophaga may lead to signs of irritation and constant preening. They appear to be more common on Norwich Fancy and formerly Lancashire Canaries which are heavily feathered breeds. Treatment as for mites will destroy such lice, which can only survive for a short time away from their host.

Pox

Canaries are particularly susceptible to a viral infection known as pox. The virus can be transmitted by biting insects such as mosquitos, and so the disease itself is often more prevalent in summer but it may also be passed directly from bird to bird. The incubation period is between three and sixteen days, with the initial sites of infection usually the eyes or legs. Within four days, yellowish lumps spread from the eyes down around the beak and over the head, also being found in the mouth itself. In the latter stages the canaries may show difficulty in breathing before death occurs.

There are, however, several strains of pox virus, with some being more severe than others, so that the symptoms are often variable. In mild cases, any birds which recover

Left: *A feather louse on the vane of a feather, with its glassy looking egg placed between the barbs.*

Facing page: *Lesions around the eyes are a common manifestation of pox, seen here on a European Goldfinch.*

will be immune to other attacks, and this underlies the principal of vaccination. Veterinary advice should be sought on this matter, but in areas of Holland and Spain where the disease occurs regularly, such preventive treatment is of great value. There is no cure for the disease once it has developed, and this virus can survive well in the environment. The scabs are thus liable to be a source of infection for other birds in the vicinity, especially when wiped off on to a perch.

The choice of a suitable disinfectant to kill the virus in the environment is therefore a very important consideration in preventing the spread of infection. Sodium hypochlorite or an iodophor preparation should prove effective, but their action is likely to be handicapped by the presence of organic matter. Thorough cleaning of the canaries' accommodation is thus recommended prior to disinfection. Advice on a suitable disinfectant can be sought from a pharmacist.

A Fife Fancy canary.

Suggested Reading

ENCYCLOPEDIA OF CANARIES by G. T. Dodwell (H-967)
The history of canary keeping introduces chapters on housing and equipment, feeding and general management, and breeding. A discussion of the breeding cycle and the accessories needed by the birds covers the practical side, while genetics, breeding strategies, and management principles deal with the theoretical aspects of canary husbandry. Chapters on further aspects of care (molting, illness, and preparation for exhibiting) precede accounts of the various breeds, which cover type, color, and song canaries, including those of North American origin.
Illustrated with 48 color and 28 black-and-white photos. Hard cover, 5½ × 8", 281 pp.

THE COMPLETE CAGE AND AVIARY BIRD HANDBOOK by David Alderton (H-1087)
Already well known for his books and articles on avicultural subjects, veterinarian David Alderton now surveys the whole field of cage and aviary birds. Treating the species by family, he provides current information on the following seed-eating birds: canaries and other selected fringillids; all the commonly available estrildid finches, with details on Zebra and Society finches; many of the whydahs and weaver finches; a sampling of the buntings and tanagers; and pigeons and quails. The psittacine sections cover Budgerigars, Cockatiels, lovebirds, and their varieties, along with a representative collection of other species. Less usual avicultural subjects are species from these groups: barbets, hornbills, toucans, bulbuls, leafbirds, babblers, thrushes, white-eyes, sunbirds, hummingbirds, mynahs, starlings, crows, and touracos. Each section contains remarks about feeding, general care, and breeding, followed by species commentaries.
Tony Tilford, who has so successfully photographed British and European birds and color canaries and other aviary birds, contributes color photographs to illustrate 167 of the species, breeds, or varieties written about. Opening with a chapter on avian biology, subsequent chapters cover birds as pets and generally discuss housing, feeding, management, illness, breeding, and the genetics of the color mutations. More than 60 drawings and 20 black-and-white photographs help the reader to visualize anatomical structures, the design of aviaries and furnishings, and the paradigms of inheritance.
Hard cover, 7½ × 9½", 160 pp.

EXHIBITING BIRDS by Dr. A. E. Decoteau (H-1036)
Written by a nationally known judge, this authoritative introduction to exhibiting and competition covers all aspects of showing birds. It describes how to prepare for a show, how a show is organized, and what to expect on the day of the show. The discussions of the Schedule of Classes and the theory and practice of judging will be helpful both to judges and to exhibitors. The final chapter looks at the standards according to which the different kinds of birds are judged.
Illustrated with 89 color and 62 black-and-white photos. Hard cover, 5½ × 8", 192 pp.

Index

Page numbers in boldface refer to illustrations.